ZEITGESCHICHTE

Ehrenpräsidentin:
em. Univ.-Prof. Dr. Erika Weinzierl († 2014)

Herausgeber:
Univ.-Prof. DDr. Oliver Rathkolb

Redaktion:
em. Univ.-Prof. Dr. Rudolf Ardelt (Linz), ao. Univ.-Prof.^{in} Mag.^{a} Dr.^{in} Ingrid Bauer (Salzburg/Wien), SSc Mag.^{a} Dr.^{in} Ingrid Böhler (Innsbruck), Dr.^{in} Lucile Dreidemy (Wien), Dr.^{in} Linda Erker (Wien), Prof. Dr. Michael Gehler (Hildesheim), ao. Univ.-Prof. i. R. Dr. Robert Hoffmann (Salzburg), ao. Univ.-Prof. Dr. Michael John / Koordination (Linz), Assoz. Prof.^{in} Dr.^{in} Birgit Kirchmayr (Linz), Dr. Oliver Kühschelm (Wien), Univ.-Prof. Dr. Ernst Langthaler (Linz), Dr.^{in} Ina Markova (Wien), Mag.^{a} Agnes Meisinger (Wien), Univ.-Prof. Mag. Dr. Wolfgang Mueller (Wien), Univ.-Prof. Dr. Bertrand Perz (Wien), Univ.-Prof. Dr. Dieter Pohl (Klagenfurt), Univ.-Prof.^{in} Dr.^{in} Margit Reiter (Salzburg), Dr.^{in} Lisa Rettl (Wien), Univ.-Prof. Mag. Dr. Dirk Rupnow (Innsbruck), Mag.^{a} Adina Seeger (Wien), Ass.-Prof. Mag. Dr. Valentin Sima (Klagenfurt), Prof.^{in} Dr.^{in} Sybille Steinbacher (Frankfurt am Main), Dr. Christian H. Stifter / Rezensionsteil (Wien), Prof. HR Mag. Markus Stumpf, MSc (Wien), Gastprof. (FH) Priv.-Doz. Mag. Dr. Wolfgang Weber, MA, MAS (Vorarlberg), Mag. Dr. Florian Wenninger (Wien), Univ.-Prof.^{in} Mag.^{a} Dr.^{in} Heidrun Zettelbauer (Graz).

Peer-Review Committee:
Ass.-Prof.^{in} Mag.^{a} Dr.^{in} Tina Bahovec (Institut für Geschichte, Universität Klagenfurt), Prof. Dr. Arnd Bauerkämper (Fachbereich Geschichts- und Kulturwissenschaften, Freie Universität Berlin), Günter Bischof, Ph.D. (Center Austria, University of New Orleans), Dr.^{in} Regina Fritz (Institut für Zeitgeschichte, Universität Wien/Historisches Institut, Universität Bern), ao. Univ.-Prof.^{in} Mag.^{a} Dr.^{in} Johanna Gehmacher (Institut für Zeitgeschichte, Universität Wien), Univ.-Prof. i. R. Dr. Ernst Hanisch (Salzburg), Univ.-Prof.^{in} Mag.^{a} Dr.^{in} Gabriella Hauch (Institut für Geschichte, Universität Wien), Univ.-Doz. Dr. Hans Heiss (Institut für Zeitgeschichte, Universität Innsbruck), Robert G. Knight, Ph.D. (Department of Politics, History and International Relations, Loughborough University), Dr.^{in} Jill Lewis (University of Wales, Swansea), Prof. Dr. Oto Luthar (Slowenische Akademie der Wissenschaften, Ljubljana), Hon.-Prof. Dr. Wolfgang Neugebauer (Dokumentationsarchiv des österreichischen Widerstandes, Wien), Mag. Dr. Peter Pirker (Institut für Zeitgeschichte, Universität Innsbruck), Prof. Dr. Markus Reisenleitner (Department of Humanities, York University, Toronto), Assoz. Prof.^{in} Dr.^{in} Elisabeth Röhrlich (Institut für Geschichte, Universität Wien), ao. Univ.-Prof.^{in} Dr.^{in} Karin M. Schmidlechner-Lienhart (Institut für Geschichte/Zeitgeschichte, Universität Graz), Univ.-Prof. i. R. Mag. Dr. Friedrich Stadler (Wien), Prof. Dr. Gerald J. Steinacher (University of Nebraska-Lincoln), Assoz.-Prof. DDr. Werner Suppanz (Institut für Geschichte/Zeitgeschichte, Universität Graz), Univ.-Prof. Dr. Philipp Ther, MA (Institut für Osteuropäische Geschichte, Universität Wien), Prof. Dr. Stefan Troebst (Leibniz-Institut für Geschichte und Kultur des östlichen Europa, Universität Leipzig), Prof. Dr. Michael Wildt (Institut für Geschichtswissenschaften, Humboldt-Universität zu Berlin), Dr.^{in} Maria Wirth (Institut für Zeitgeschichte, Universität Wien).

zeitgeschichte
51. Jg., Heft 3 (2024)

To Help or Not to Help – Humanitarianism in the 20th Century

Edited by
Sarah Knoll and Katharina Seibert

V&R unipress

Vienna University Press

Contents

Sarah Knoll / Katharina Seibert
Editorial 309

Articles

Doina Anca Cretu
The American Red Cross and Visions of Rebuilding of the Balkans after
the First World War 313

Katharina Seibert
Springboards for Women's Careers. International Humanitarianism,
the Spanish Civil War, and the Rise of Mercedes Milá Nolla 335

Julia Schulte-Werning
Milk for the Mellah. Infant Health and the Logistics of Post-Holocaust
Humanitarian Aid for Jewish Communities in French Morocco 359

Sarah Knoll
Humanitarianism as a Policy Strategy? Revisiting Austria's
'Humanitarian Tradition' 381

Abstracts 403

Reviews

Lisa Gottschall
Zuzana Panczová/Gabriela Kiliánová/Tomáš Kubisa, Volkskunde in den
Diensten des Dritten Reiches. Deutsche Forscher und Forscherinnen in
der Slowakei 409

Nikolaus Lehner
Raoul Kneucker/Manfried Welan, Die Fragen des Pilatus. Wahrheit
– Gerechtigkeit – Glaube 412

Authors 415

Sarah Knoll / Katharina Seibert

Editorial

Today, humanitarianism, as a moral imperative to help, is prevalent, especially in the so-called Western world. The public reacts to natural disasters, war, or medical emergencies with a desire to alleviate suffering. People donate money, stars act as humanitarian ambassadors, and states include funds in their national budgets. In the current situation with the ongoing wars in Gaza and Ukraine, or the hunger epidemic in Sudan, the public awareness for humanitarian action is once again heightened. Since the late 1800s, the term "humanitarianism" has been used for a variety of social movements, activities, and organizations.[1] Today, what began as a desire to humanize warfare encompasses the fight against poverty through technical assistance and support for refugees. To this day, in the public perception, humanitarianism is often understood as apolitical and benevolent, as exemplified by the Oxford English Dictionary's definition when it highlights the "concern for human welfare as a primary or pre-eminent moral good; action, or disposition to act, on the basis of this concern rather than for pragmatic or strategic reasons."[2] In recent decades, historians of humanitarianism have rightly criticized that the history of humanitarianism has long catered to this image of benevolence. These historians have begun to critically assess humanitarian organizations, politics, and the motives of humanitarian actors. As Michael Barnett stated in *Empire of Humanity*, humanitarianism is "about meeting the needs of others and meeting your own needs."[3] In other words, humanitarian aid thus evolves in a tense dialectic between people in need and the individual agendas of the 'benevolent saviors.'

The papers in this special issue approach humanitarianism and humanitarian aid from the perspective of such 'benevolent saviors' and their agendas, and cover

---
1 Peter J. Hoffman and Thomas G. Weiss, *Humanitarianism, War, and Politics. Solferino to Syria and Beyond* (Lanham/Boulder/New York/London: Rowman & Littlefield, 2018), 4.
2 Humanitarianism, Oxford English Dictionary 2009, https://www.oed.com/dictionary/humanitarianism_n?tab=meaning_and_use&tl=true#1126648 (23 February 2024).
3 Michael Barnett, *Empire of Humanity: A History of Humanitarianism* (Ithaca, NY: Cornell University Press, 2011), 14.

different moments in history and geographical regions in the 20th century. What motivated these humanitarian actors? What goals were associated with their missions? How did humanitarian agendas merge with collective imaginaries and aims? In the spotlight are aid workers of the American Red Cross who set out to rebuild the Balkans after the First World War (Anca Doina Cretus), a Spanish nurse who used the networks and opportunities humanitarianism offered her to build herself a career during the Spanish Civil War (Katharina Seibert), various Jewish relief organizations that competed for authority while trying to relieve malnutrition in the *mellah* of Casablanca after the Holocaust (Julia Schulte-Werning), and the Austrian state and society in their process of forging Austria's 'humanitarian tradition' during the Cold War (Sarah Knoll). Humanitarianism is thus analyzed by the authors of these papers as a means to vernacularizing a reconstruction mission according to civilizing desires (ARC), as an enabling factor for individual professionalization (Spain), as a power struggle (Morocco), and as a tool for domestic and international policymaking (Austria).

Articles

Doina Anca Cretu

The American Red Cross and Visions of Rebuilding of the Balkans after the First World War

I. Introduction

"No part of Europe needs rebuilding so much as the Balkans. It was the conflict between Slav and Teuton in this region which was the primary cause of this war. There can never be a stable peace here while the Balkans remain turbulent as they have been […]. So it is to the interest not only of Europeans, but to the interest as well of all Americans who want to avoid […] another Chateau Thierry [sic], that the Balkans be stabilized."[1]

This was the assessment of Gregory Mason, a field journalist, in the American newspaper *The Outlook* after an investigative trip to the Balkans. The article, suggestively titled "The Red Cross Rebuilding the Balkans," claimed to shed light on the work and the vital importance of the American Red Cross (ARC) in the region. The humanitarian organization had long counted on the press to describe and paint an image of their aid work in belligerent Europe during the First World War.[2] At home, this method was intended to raise awareness and funds. In locales of aid reception, ARC used the media to tell people what was fundamentally being done on their behalf in order to gain support.[3] In this context, Mason's interpretation of its work was, perhaps unsurprisingly, aligned with ARC's own projects, the Balkans becoming the potential cradle of *humanitarianism as emergency relief* and *humanitarianism as rebuilding*.

ARC became a staple of the humanitarian landscape in Europe during the First World War. It was established in 1881, under the presidency of Clara Barton, a

---

I would like to thank Sarah Knoll and Katharina Seibert for their efforts in putting this special issue together and for their advice during the development of this essay. I am further grateful to Rok Stergar for his feedback on initial drafts of the article.

1 Gregory Mason, "The Red Cross Rebuilding the Balkans," *The Outlook*. Taken from Commission to the Balkans, RG 200, Box 895, Central File 1917–1934, Records of the American National Red Cross, National Archives and Records Administration (NARA), College Park, MD., USA.
2 Report of Balkan Commission and its Sub-Commissions, Vol. 1, 1918–1919, RG 200, Box 893, Records of the American Red Cross, NARA, College Park, MD., USA.
3 Ibid.

schoolteacher from Oxford, Massachusetts, against a backdrop of expanded American Protestant missionary activities. Prior to the First World War, ARC focused its work primarily on domestic assistance. However, the US government sanctioned its humanitarian interventions in Cuba during the Spanish–American War of 1898 and to Mexico at the time of the revolution there in 1910.[4] These missions abroad, however, had been small scale. It was the First World War that gave ARC ample opportunity to assist people in a high-magnitude operation abroad, with financial and governmental support at home. At first, ARC's wartime humanitarianism focused on relief of Western Europe, paying specific attention to stabilizing France and Italy through material aid.[5] However, once the war ended, ARC re-routed most of its assistance in Central and Eastern Europe, the Near East, and, indeed, the Balkans.

This article looks at ARC's language and practices of humanitarianism in the Balkans in the first months after the First World War. It particularly pays attention to the Balkan Commission, an umbrella branch of ARC, established on 1 November 1918. Under this singular entity, local commissions were present in Greece and South Serbia from the outset, followed by other units located in North Serbia, Albania, Montenegro, Bosnia and Herzegovina, and Romania. Over 500 American volunteers (i.e. doctors, nurses, and other administrative personnel) were stationed in larger cities and towns across different countries, with aid practices radiating to rural areas too.[6]

In recent years, historians have highlighted the nexus between relief and rehabilitation in the First World War era. In a rebuttal of the argument that humanitarianism with a long-term agenda was fundamentally a product of the period after the Second World War, various studies have pointed to how relief workers envisioned their praxis as intentionally transformative in the long term after the First World War.[7] Emergency relief was thus bridged with (re-)construction. I build on and maintain a dialogue with these works as I show that ARC's Balkan Commission encapsulated this vision by bridging emergency with

---

4 Branden Little, "Band of Crusaders: American Humanitarians, the Great War, and the Remaking of the World," unpublished PhD. thesis, University of California, Berkeley, 2009, 117.
5 Julia Irwin, "Nation Building and Rebuilding: The American Red Cross in Italy during the Great War," *The Journal of the Gilded Age and Progressive Era* 8 (2009) 3: 407–39; Michael E. McGuire, "At (Red) cross purposes: American Red Cross humanitarian "arrogance" and France's Great War relief and reconstruction, 1917–20," *European Review of History: Revue européene d'histoire* 30 (2022) 5: 705–26.
6 Lieut. Col. Henry W. Anderson, "Review of the Work of the Various Commissions," Report of the Balkan Commission and its Sub-commissions, Vol.1, 1918–1919, RG 200, Box 893, NARA, College Park, MD., USA.
7 See for example Silvia Salvatici, *A History of Humanitarianism, 1755–1989* (Manchester, UK: Manchester University Press, 2019); Davide Rodogno, *Night on Earth: A History of International Humanitarianism in the Near East, 1918–1930* (Cambridge, UK: Cambridge University Press, 2021).

"constructive" work. It first addressed the urgent needs that the war produced, such as food supplies or medical assistance. However, the American organization's leaders and its workers in the field sought a new reconstructive scope to their work, through construction of long-term infrastructure, education, or training in American methods in healthcare.

I argue here that notions of Balkanism shaped the language and agendas of ARC's humanitarianism driven through the Balkan Commission in the region. I rely conceptually on Maria Todorova's well-known interpretation of Balkanism as not merely a sub-species of Orientalism but rather a measure of "otherness" in and of itself. According to Todorova's understanding, the broadly defined "Balkans" have long been perceived as "the other" from a political, ideological, and cultural perspective and "have served as a repository of negative characteristics against which a positive and self-congratulatory image of the 'European' and 'the west' has been constructed." And as Todorova points out, Balkanism has exempted "the west" from accusations of racism, colonialism, or Christian intolerance: after all, the people of the Balkans are European enough, white enough, and Christian enough.[8]

In this context, I suggest that ARC humanitarians conceived of their work in the Balkans through two lenses: on one hand, there was the organic suffering caused by war – its violence and its socio-economic effects. On the other hand, the organization's leaders and relief workers held assumptions that Balkan people had Oriental features and behaviors due to the Ottoman rule that pervaded European territories, European people, and a long European history. Departing from this, ideas of stabilization and civilization thus became embedded in ARC's humanitarian language and the aid agendas that leaders and workers on the ground drew up for this region. In the eyes of American humanitarians, the Balkans were victims, and the Balkans were primitive; at the same time, the Balkans were fixable due to their inherent Europeanness and their whiteness. Thus, in my interpretation, humanitarians' *Balkanist* discourse entailed a recognition of this region and of these people as European. They assumed that it was rather the forcefully Orientalist intervention in their lives through Ottoman rule that eventually led to the backwardness of their living conditions, which were largely rural and lacking hygiene and education. In this context, relief workers believed that with American assistance, not only would suffering as a result of the war be alleviated, but alternatives in lifestyle would eventually lead to these people's "westernized" civilization.

---

8 Maria Todorova, "The Balkans: From Discovery to Invention," *Slavic Review* 53 (1994) 2: 453–82; for the magnum opus on the topic, see Maria Todorova, *Imagining the Balkans* (Oxford, UK: Oxford University Press, 2002).

This relationship between humanitarianism and Balkanism is at the center of the article and also serves as a lens into broader debates about *deservingness of aid* and how relief workers or leaders of aid institutions conceptualized suffering and need. Narratives and perceptions of suffering generate a mobilization of empathy that has driven humanitarian processes.[9] The First World War established a backdrop of disaster that enabled mobilization of resources for what Luc Boltanski notoriously called "distant suffering." However, for ARC humanitarians, need was caused not merely by war and its precipitous effects, but also by the protracted imperial rule that had rendered people helpless, lacking autonomy, and, by extension, susceptible to various political dangers and social anarchy.

I methodologically anchor my analysis in humanitarians' point of view as I dissect the language and repertoires of aid, as well as aspects of its practical implementation, through the reports and notes found in the archives of ARC. I move my narrative in and out of different locales – cities, towns, villages – that were targets of the Balkan Commission more broadly. But in so doing, I explore humanitarians' own maps, definitions, and interpretations of "the Balkans." It is important to note that this is a non-prescriptive approach to the oft-contentious meaning and understanding of what the "Balkans" represent. Humanitarians followed their own borders and geographies. In this vein, historian Davide Rodogno has highlighted the idea of aid givers' "mental maps" that were infused with assumptions about civilization and lack thereof; this, relief workers thought, functioned according to geographic, ethnic, and religious beliefs that shaped lacunae of modernity in various sites of aid reception.[10]

Overall, this is an exploration of how ARC humanitarians envisioned the different facets of rebuilding in the Balkans. I do not suggest here that this region constituted the postwar financial *foci* of American humanitarianism. In fact, the amount of aid that the Balkan Commission employed was often limited when faced with bigger projects of assistance across Europe and relatively patchily administered. I focus on what motivated ARC humanitarians to work in the Balkans, assumptions regarding this region, perceptions of local encounters, and varied beliefs regarding multiple facets of need.

This article first follows what historian Keith Watenpaugh described as "humanitarian imaginations"[11] of the Balkans. Here, I emphasize relief workers' perceptions and constructions of humanitarian need in this region. It is difficult

---

9 See Richard Ashby Wilson and Richard D. Brown, "Introduction," in *Humanitarianism and Suffering: The Mobilization of Empathy,* edited by Richard Ashby Wilson and Richard D. Brown (Cambridge, UK: Cambridge University Press, 2011), 1–28.
10 Rodogno, *Night on Earth*, 3.
11 Keith David Watenpaugh, *Bread from Stones: The Middle East and the Making of Modern Humanitarianism* (Berkeley, CA: University of California Press, 2015), 33.

to assess the exact knowledge that individual ARC humanitarians and the organization's leaders had of the Balkans prior to the war. However, as this first section shows, by the time of their arrival, humanitarians saw the Balkans as a cradle of violence, primitivism, and suffering. And, more importantly, for ARC humanitarians, they meant realms of possibility for aid to function and rebuild. In practical terms, this meant relief and various ambitions and practices of reconstruction, the themes of the following two sections. ARC leaders and workers approached aid-giving gradually: initially, there was the urgency caused by war destruction that had to be addressed. This meant relief in the form of healthcare and food in the name of people's stabilization on an emergency basis. In the process, as the second section of this article will show, they became convinced they could inculcate notions of cleanliness or benefits of nutrition to people who presumably knew little of either. Once the war ended and the immediacy of assistance waned, ARC shifted its attention to reconstructive ambitions and the long-term imprint that humanitarianism would and could leave in the Balkans. In this context, the third section of this article focuses on the *problématique* of orphan care as a central peacetime ARC agenda that would mesh a Balkanist discourse, urgent pragmaticism, and a civilizational approach to suffering and want in this region.

II. The Balkans in Humanitarian Imaginations

In January 1919, Sara McCarron, one of the many ARC relief workers who had volunteered to assist various war sufferers, travelled to Podgorica, the largest town in Montenegro. She held a specific target: addressing conditions in schools and assisting school children with food, medicine, and healthcare, as well as providing clothing for those in need. McCarron described her mission in the Balkans as an adventure in and of itself. In this way, she echoed the writings of travelers from decades before, who wrote of new discoveries and racial and geographic archetypes. "It was the most thrilling ride we ever had to expect to have," wrote McCarron on her first encounters with Montenegro. The dirty roads of various villages she wrote about were, however, a mere backdrop to the broader humanitarian imagination that McCarron's report reveals. The often harsh landscape of the Balkans contoured an environment that augmented wartime suffering, poverty, and Oriental imagery. In this context, McCarron imagined her humanitarian agenda as providing an alternative to the lives of the people she encountered in her adventures. Her mental map of suffering and need was anchored in Oriental-like towns where people of different ethnicities and religions, but with a common "low morale" (in McCarron's words) and little to live on, waited for help. This is what a part of her report recognized:

"My district was in the old town – Turkish district. We called it "Turkey-town." It was 500 years old. The spirit of the people was at a low ebb when we first arrived. They were slow in grasping the idea that we were there to help them, but when they did, every door was opened – Christian and Turkish alike – and they appreciated everything that was done for them. The poverty was terrible – no fires in some of the homes; scantily clad; dirty; no soap; hungry – many times I found them on the floor wrapped in a bundle of dirty rags to keep them warm – so dirty you would almost be afraid to touch them. Many of them had no beds. Some had some mattresses to put on the floor – they were well off. Others, desperately poor cases, just had a slip of burlap to lie on. Oh! It was heart-rending."[12]

McCarron's writings on her discovery of Podgorica are an edifying example of ways ARC humanitarians thought of their rapport with the Balkan recipient region and the people living there. In this sense, relief workers developed an imagination of need that brought together war suffering and what I have previously called *remediable primitivism*. Scholars have long pointed to humanitarian processes as arenas of inequality that confer power to the givers when they have rapport with the needy humanitarians. For example, Davide Rodogno has written on humanitarians' inherent need for "chaos to harbinger order. They needed anarchy to govern, the needy to rescue, and war and horror to exist."[13] From this understanding, the so-called Balkans were the quintessential place of humanitarian mobilization and transfer of assistance: here, war brought suffering; collapse of empires brought feeble sovereignties and measures of governance, and thus anarchy was possible.

On the other hand, in his writings on the making of international humanitarianism in the Middle East, Keith Watenpaugh has highlighted that the meaning of "need" is fundamentally malleable and thus humanitarian imaginations are not built on the severity of suffering alone. Need, and thus *deservingness*, is also about historical encounters and humanitarians' subjectivities, about civilizational narratives, and, ultimately, about what truly shapes empathy in a successful manner.[14] In this understanding, need is subjective, organic, and constructed. In this context, I posit, Balkanism entered ARC humanitarians' imagination in terms of war events and related suffering. But even more so, it shaped the deservingness of aid recipients through pre-defined perceptions of

---

12 Sara McCarron, "District School Work in Montenegro," Commission to Montenegro, RG 200, Box 907, Central File 1917–1934, Records of the American National Red Cross, NARA, College Park, MD., USA.
13 Davide Rodogno, "Certainty, compassion and the ingrained arrogance of humanitarians," in *The Red Cross Movement: Myths, practices, turning points*, edited by Neville Wylie, Melanie Oppenheimer, and James Crossland (Manchester, UK: Manchester University Press, 2020), 33.
14 Watenpaugh, *Bread from Stones*, 33.

Orientalism *qua* primitivism and humanitarians' beliefs in the need to stabilize the region in the name of European peace.

Ideas of protracted suffering because of war in the Balkans infused the American humanitarian imagination. Prior to the First World War, in the nineteenth century, there were wars of independence that put this region on the humanitarian map of the so-called West.[15] Furthermore, in 1913, the Carnegie Endowment for International Peace published a report on the Balkan Wars of 1912-1913. Produced by eight politicians, professors, or journalists from France, the US, Great Britain, Russia, Germany, and Austria-Hungary, the report sought to "inquire the causes and conduct of the Balkan wars." It detailed historical roots of the conflict in the Balkans, presented varied analyses and points of view, and mapped aspirations of belligerents in the normative frameworks of international law. "What then is the duty of the civilized world in the Balkans [...]?" asked the report regarding the moral and social consequences of the wars.[16] The answer to this question lay in the exposure and, indeed, imposition of legal frameworks such as arbitration treaties and judicial settlements of international disputes. But beyond the meanings of interventionist forms of international law as measures of a civilizing process for the Balkans, the Carnegie Endowment for International Peace report framed the meaning of this region as a site of war and violence. Furthermore, it contoured the place of the Balkans at the interface of the civilized West and the non-civilized East.

The vision of the Balkans as eaten by conflict, violence and its effects, such as food scarcity, was a common point of the mental maps that ARC humanitarians contoured regarding the potential for aid to shift people's fates in this region. As mentioned before, it is difficult to trace humanitarians' individual knowledge and understanding of the Balkans before their arrival. It is possible to consider, however, that prior wars and battles coupled with the start of the First World War shaped American humanitarians' assumptions regarding the people of the Balkans as the quintessential war sufferers. Accordingly, on-the-ground violence mattered, but there were also indirect effects of war that fundamentally altered Balkan peoples' lives. It was an idea that circulated early also in the reports and writings of the ARC leadership. For example, Ernest P. Bicknell, the head of ARC during the war, embarked on a Europe-wide trip to survey the conditions that his organization could address. For Bicknell, the situation in Serbia was to receive the

---

15 See for example Fabian Klose, "'The emergence of humanitarian intervention: three centuries of 'enforcing humanity,'" in *The Emergence of Humanitarian Intervention: Ideas and Practice from the Nineteenth Century to the Present*, edited by Fabian Klose (Cambridge, UK: Cambridge University Press, 2016), 1–29.
16 Carnegie Endowment for International Peace, Division of Intercourse and Education, *Report of the International Commission to Inquire into the Causes and Conduct of the Balkan Wars* (Washington, DC: Carnegie Endowment for International Peace, 1914), 273.

utmost attention due to its suffering under Turkish rule, its fight for independence in 1912–1913, the start of the First World War, and a fully-fledged typhus epidemic that curtailed potential advancement and generated social and political collapse.[17]

The issue of Balkan primitivism and American aid as a path to civilization molded humanitarian imagination regarding the meaning and the potential of this region in this era of the First World War. Ideas of people's rather long-term war suffering fed into the conceptualization of ARC's humanitarianism as emergency means from the outset. However, this was coupled with ideas of American humanitarianism as means towards a distinctly Western vision of civilization. As Maria Todorova or Larry Wolff noted, the Balkans as a site of primitivism had long been a trope that travel writers, diplomats, or politicians had observed primarily since the nineteenth century.[18] In this vein, ARC leaders as well as relief workers on the ground imagined the objects of their assistance at the intersection of Europeanness and Orientalism manifested through lack of education, poverty and dirtiness, and, at times, poor governance. It was an idea that Ernest P. Bicknell, once more, circulated early on, in his initial surveys of the region. Writing on the suffering Serbs, he claimed that they appeared to be "strong, simple, kind, independent, and homeloving, although not yet developed by education and experience to a high order of ability in the organization of complex public or private affairs."[19]

Humanitarian elites believed that at the heart of Balkan backwardness lay the long-term imperial, and especially Ottoman rule in parts of the region. Ideas of "Mohammedans'" lack of civilization pervaded much of the humanitarian language as organizations transferred relief work also in the Near East, as well as in the Middle East more generally.[20] They certainly believed that Ottoman populations were uncivilized and unable to govern themselves. It was an idea that also was at the heart of Woodrow Wilson's own animosities towards the Ottoman Empire and Turks at large.[21] Indeed, as Larry Wolff has shown, Wilson endorsed ideas of the abolition of the Ottoman Empire and the Turks' removal from Europe on the basis of a perceived violent rule and antagonism towards Western civilization.[22]

---

17 Ernest P. Bicknell, "The Genial and Popular General Popovitch," *The Red Cross Courier*, August 1936.
18 Todorova, *Imagining the Balkans*; Larry Wolff, *Inventing Eastern Europe: The Map of Civilization on the Mind of the Enlightenment* (Stanford, CA: Stanford University Press, 1996).
19 Bicknell, "The Genial and Popular General Popovitch."
20 Rodogno, *Night on Earth*; Melanie S. Tanielian, *The Charity of War: Famine, Humanitarian Aid, and World War I in the Middle East* (Stanford, CA: Stanford University Press, 2017).
21 Rodogno, *Night on Earth*, 57.
22 Larry Wolff, *Woodrow Wilson and the Reimagining of Eastern Europe* (Stanford, CA: Stanford University Press, 2020), 15–55.

For some ARC humanitarians, the presence of Muslim populations in parts that had been under Ottoman rule was a reported surprise, echoing an initially murky understanding of the sociopolitical and cultural realm they operated in; but once they arrived, it also became a central factor in the framing of the need for aid in the Balkans. One report on Bosnia and Herzegovina signaled that Muslim populations were, in fact, the majority: "At Mostar, nearly half of the population is composed of Mohammedans, and at Sarajevo out of a population of 55,000 over 20,000 are Mohameddans [sic]."[23] The numbers were one thing. But what was evident in humanitarians' eyes was the inherent primitivism that this majority Muslim population brought with it. It is possible that this was due to ARC humanitarians' limited prior knowledge regarding the complex political constellation of the Balkans. The Ottoman Empire had ruled Bosnia until 1878, when a series of peasant uprisings and international conflicts forced cessation of control and transfer to the Habsburg Monarchy. Invoking the international mandate to occupy and "civilize" the province, Austria-Hungary administered Bosnia from 1878.[24] It was a convoluted governance that ARC humanitarians interpreted in terms of competing levels of civilization. Thus, they made distinctions according to their perceptions of advancement rather than an overarching anti-imperial language. In this sense, they claimed that "under the Turkish rule, Bosnia Herzegovina was in deplorable backward condition," whereas the Austrian administration "set itself intelligently to the material development of the provinces, so that by 1914, Bosnia Herzegovina had reached a relatively high degree of prosperity."[25] At the same time, they claimed that the Ottomans' tentacles shifted the ethnic profile of the people in Bosnia and Herzegovina and, by extension, shifted behaviors. "The Turks, as they are called, are really Slavs who became Mohameddans, and have become almost like a different race. They are noted for laziness and dirtiness. Their women never work for a living, but the old ones do not hesitate to adopt begging as a profession,"[26] the same report noted of social and behavioral limitations along declared racial lines.

In ARC humanitarians' imagination of the Balkans, the Ottoman-infused Orientalism separated people of this region from a fully European identity. And,

---

23 George B. Ford, "Bosnia and Herzegovina: Historical Facts relating to the Work of the American Red Cross in Bosnia and Herzgovina up to September 15, 1919," Commission to Serbia, Box 895, RG 200, Central File 1917–1934, Records of the American National Red Cross, NARA, College Park, MD., USA.
24 Edin Hajdarpasic, *Whose Bosnia? Nationalism and Political Imagination in the Balkans, 1840–1914* (Ithaca, NY: Cornell University Press, 2015), 176.
25 Ford, "Bosnia and Herzegovina: Historical Facts relating to the Work of the American Red Cross in Bosnia and Herzgovina up to September 15, 1919."
26 Henry W. Anderson letter to Robert E. Olds, 26 March 1919, Commission to the Balkans, RG 200, Box 895, Central File 1917–1934, Records of the American National Red Cross, NARA, College Park, MD., USA.

accordingly, it was certainly what separated them from the American way of life in some relief workers' assessments. Thus reflected Elizabeth Freeman, an assistant to ARC Balkans medical officer, as she traveled to various Serbian districts and provinces in order to survey needs and deliveries of aid:

> "The isolated farmhouse of America, sign of security and a country at peace, is unknown in these troubled communities where the little towns father their people in at sundown both for society and protection. [...] Where property is unsafe, improvement is bound to be slow, and under Turkish rule, every man's property was subject to confiscation. Why build a new house if you may never live in it? Why plant fruit trees for your masters to cut down? Why wear decent clothing if it only invites increased taxation?"[27]

Freeman sketched the potential for ARC to help the people of the Balkans to find their lost autonomy. In this sense, she suggested that ARC's brand of humanitarianism was a way to counter the limitations that these people experienced under imperial rule, even if change was to be slow.

However, not all relief workers held cautious beliefs in the capacity of the Balkans to slowly advance once given the opportunity. Some certainly thought that their recipients had to be receptive for every aid project as a measure of a civilizing agenda to work. ARC aid workers thought that the people of the Balkans were backward due to *coercive* rule by the Turks. However, they also held enough European standards for any American presence to have a potent response. For them, potential was related to Balkan people's fundamental Europeanness rather than their Orientalism and, by extension, to their openness to an American brand of modernity. It was an idea of redeemability that rendered humanitarianism with both a short- and a long-term agenda useful and, by extension, made these people deserving of assistance.

I argue that ARC workers conceived redeemability through the lens of their recipients' openness to their presence, the possible conditions of their aid-giving, and the general potential for these people to overcome precariousness. This was evident in the case of reported interactions with Serbs, for example, who were described as "self-respecting people" open to "enabl[ing] the American visitors to secure as precisely as possible the information they desired."[28] At the same time, the same Serbs were portrayed as being of barely educated, especially in rural areas, but "active-minded, interested in things, and responsible to new

---

27 Mrs. J.K. Freeman to Colonel H.W. Anderson, "Report on Serbia," 18 June 1919, Commission to the Balkans, Central File 1917–1934, RG 200, Box 895, Records of the American National Red Cross, NARA, College Park, MD., USA.
28 "Serbia: Preliminary Memorandum Submitted to Lieut. Col. Harvey D. Gibson, Chairman of the American Red Cross Commission in Europe, by Lieut. Col. Homer Folks and Staff," 22 January 1919, , Commission to the Balkans, RG 200, Box 905, Central File 1917–1934, Records of the American National Red Cross, NARA, College Park, MD., USA.

ideas and methods."[29] In similar terms, an account wrote of the people of Montenegro, where humanitarians believed that a "child-like cordiality" truly enabled the "possibility for successful work in Montenegro. We must not fail them at this time, for it is in our power to help these people to start a new and more prosperous country, which will fit in better in the picture we would like to create of the Balkan States," this report noted while connecting ARC's brand of humanitarianism to bigger and broader changes to the region and its states.[30]

For ARC humanitarians, the perceived Europeanness of the Balkans further trumped any effects of the long Turkish rule. These were ideas that, in Maria Todorova's terms, connected notions of Balkanism to both the limitations *and* the potential of ARC assistance. Humanitarians attached to this organization relied on the majoritarian whiteness and Christian religion as counters to the Orientalism that Ottomans had imprinted in this region. Mentions of a superior civilization in antiquity in areas of Macedonia or Albania demonstrated humanitarians' belief in the inborn superiority of these people that had succumbed to bigger forces. As one report about Macedonia wrote: "Once in a while one catches a glimmer of ancient Greek civilization of 500 years ago, but by contrast it makes one realize how well the Turks have succeeded in their efforts to keep this country in darkness."[31] Against this backdrop, in their humanitarian imagination, ARC relief workers posited their work in relation to alleviating long-term suffering under imperial rule while bolstering a civilization that had been suppressed.

ARC relief workers' humanitarian imagination framed the need and deservingness of people living in the Balkans in terms of war, violence, and suffering, as well as in their Orientalism and, finally, their Europeanness. For ARC humanitarians, the people's prosperity and hence their civilization had been yielded by long-term "Turkish" rule. At the same time, humanitarians believed, these people had enough potential to be receptive to an American brand of aid. These were ideas that lay at the heart of the blueprint of praxis as ARC leadership and workers on the ground developed a vision of rebuilding through emergency relief and ambitions of reconstruction with long-term effects in the region.

---

29 "Serbia: Preliminary Memorandum."
30 Col. Olds Letter to Chief Nurse, "Report on Nursing Situation in the Balkan States," Commission to the Balkans, RG 200, Box 895, Central File 1917–1934, Records of the American National Red Cross, NARA, College Park, MD., USA.
31 Mrs. J.K. Freeman to Col. Anderson, 13 June 1919, Commission to the Balkans, RG 200, Box 904, Central File 1917–1934, Records of the American National Red Cross, NARA, College Park, MD., USA.

III. Wartime Suffering and Emergency Relief

In his 1919 article for *The Outlook*, George Mason passionately wrote of the way ARC approached its work in the Balkans in the context of the war:

> "Every general knows that when you destroy the morale of the civilians behind an army, you have beaten the army. The morale of all the Balkan peoples is very low. (We are concerned here, of course, mainly with the four Balkan states which were with us in the war: Montenegro, Roumania [sic], Greece and Servia [sic]). Before the Balkans can be rebuilt on a sounder political and social basis the morale of their inhabitants must be restored. The first thing to do is to see that these people get food and clothing."[32]

With these words, Mason encapsulated the declared *raison d'être* for ARC and for other American humanitarian organizations at the time. Saving people's bodies through food relief, medical care, or clothing was tied into the saving of the mind for war sufferers.[33] In this sense, in the case of Balkan recipients, their deservingness was defined through their organic suffering dictated by the direct and indirect effects of war: destitution, displacement, and the destruction of human and physical infrastructure. Thus, the vision of rebuilding entailed bringing an initial material stabilization to those who had suffered because of the war.

ARC's humanitarian work on an emergency basis started off with small missions in Serbia and in Romania during the war. Surgical units departed to belligerent Europe as early as 1914, and Serbia was one of the locales targeted by these volunteers. However, reports of some of these workers noted that it was almost impossible to perform surgical operations in Serbia due to a lack of any infrastructure, what little existed being heavily dilapidated due to the war.[34] Furthermore, the typhus epidemic caused the most chaos in ARC's attempts to work in Serbia, as a large number of medical practitioners succumbed to the disease.[35] In this context, an ARC Serbian commission focused primarily on disease and epidemics more generally during the war,[36] with Bicknell further encouraging British, French, and Russian agencies, as well as the Rockefeller Foundation, to combine efforts and contribute money, equipment, supplies, and the services of physicians.[37]

---

32 Mason, "The Red Cross Rebuilding the Balkans."
33 Irwin, *Making the World Safe*, 167.
34 "American Red Cross Personnel Engaged in Work in Serbia During the Present War," 1 December 1919, Serbia Relief Unit, G1, Box 42, Records of the American National Red Cross, NARA, College Park, MD., USA.
35 E.F. Butler to Patterson, 10 June 1915, Serbia Relief Unit, G1, Box 42, Records of the American National Red Cross, NARA, College Park, MD., USA.
36 Little, "Band of Crusaders," 160.
37 Ibid., 245.

Concomitant to the mobilization of ARC resources to combat the aggressive spread of typhus, Romania entered the war on the side of the Allies in 1916. By 1917, an exploratory ARC mission had arrived in this country in the context of famine among the population. A difficult winter, the collapse of agrarian economy, poor infrastructure, and especially the effects of a German occupation that entailed resource extraction all contributed to extreme food scarcity.[38] ARC responded to a targeted appeal from Romania's royal family, Romanian politicians and medical experts, and American diplomats, such as Charles Vopicka, the US plenipotentiary minister in Bucharest.[39] A small commission comprising "able and experienced doctors and nurses" thus arrived in Romania with medical supplies, serums, vaccines, and food to abate epidemics as in Serbia and to alleviate hunger among the suffering population.[40]

Nevertheless, the work in both Romania and Serbia remained relatively small scale at the time, largely due to the high attention the American humanitarians paid to the war-ravaged Western European Allies. As mentioned above, most relief work and financial resources were anchored in assisting Italy or France and their civilians. Financial resources, most of which came through fundraising, seldom fell outside this geographic scope during the war. However, once most of the violence ended in 1918, ARC turned its attention to the "shatterzones of empires,"[41] namely the Near East, Central and Eastern Europe, and, finally, the Balkans. There, through the organization of the Balkan Commission in November 1918, ARC humanitarians shifted parts of its material aid capacity into medical care and food provision. Below, a few snapshots provide an insight into the ways ARC organized and conceptualized emergency assistance in the Balkans through its umbrella commission and local units that addressed medical emergencies and food scarcity.

First, medical assistance remained one of the central pillars of ARC's postwar humanitarian work in the Balkans, in a continuation of the smaller-scale wartime

---

38 See for example David Hamlin, *Germany's Empire in the East: Germans and Romania in an Era of Globalization and Total War* (Cambridge, UK: Cambridge University Press, 2017); Gheorghe Ionesco-Sisesti, *L'agriculture de la Roumanie pendant la Guerre* (Paris: Less Presses Universitaires de France, 1929).
39 Alexandru Constantinescu, Aide-Mémoire for the American Red Cross, 6 September 1917, RG 200, Box 896, Records of the American Red Cross, NARA, College Park, MD., USA; Mr. Wadsworth Letter to Ernest Bicknell, 25 April 1917, RG 200, Box 896, Records of the American Red Cross, NARA, College Park, MD., USA; Ernest Bicknell, "Rumania Strives to Keep Neutral," *The Red Cross Courier*, March 1936. Found in The Courier, Box 447, Records of the American Red Cross, NARA, College Park, MD.
40 Red Cross War Council Letter to the Department of State, 21 July 1917, RG 200, Box 896, Records of the American Red Cross, NARA, College Park, MD., USA.
41 Term from Omer Bartov and Eric D. Weitz (eds.), *Shatterzones of Empires: Coexistence and Violence in the German, Habsburg, Russian, and Ottoman Borderlands* (Bloomington, IN: Indiana University Press, 2013).

missions in Serbia and Romania. The crisis that typhus generated in Serbia during the war alerted relief workers to the need to invest in curative measures in the context of epidemics. Therefore, ARC focused much of its work on establishing medical stations in various locales across the Balkans. In Skoplje/Skopje,[42] for instance, a medical station was established immediately after the formation of the Balkan Commission in November 1918. Then one of the largest towns in Serbia, Skoplje/Skopje became one of the centers of American relief activities. ARC humanitarians' specific attention to this town was motivated by the extreme suffering caused by the war and Bulgarian occupation. Indeed, much like in the case of Romania during the war, food scarcity, pillaged houses, and general deprivation were related to the spread of epidemics among emaciated people. In this context, ARC paid particular attention to healthcare, claiming that epidemics and poor health were primarily related to the conditions and consequences of war.[43]

Typhus also remained a significant crisis to the work of the Balkan Commission. In wartime Serbia, humanitarians addressed the epidemic within the context of the conflict. In peacetime, however, ARC relief workers sidelined the effects of the conflagration and framed the spreading of disease along racial, ethnic, and religious lines. In this context, the Muslim population of the Balkans were deemed both the carriers and main sufferers of typhus due to their backward ways of life. Driven by specific beliefs that "Mohammetans" (sic) were not clean, lacked clothing, and did not possess an understanding of the very basic rules of hygiene, ARC relief workers connected assistance for those suffering from typhus and typhus control as addressing the inherent cultural and social backwardness of these seemingly Oriental people. This was the logic behind ARC's targeted control of a typhus crisis in Bosnia and Herzegovina. "The question of cleaning up these two countries is not one of treating the sick but of delousing a country with 2,000,000 inhabitants," wrote one proposal for aid work in this region. The note requested ten doctors, including women physicians, disinfectants, powders and fluids, sterilizers, and house disinfectors, as well as propaganda work to make the presence of ARC palatable to their recipients. In an instance of planned transfer of models, reports wrote of a potential approach similar to "Swat the Fly" campaign trialed and tested in the US in 1917; at that time, the housefly was identified as the cause of polio, typhoid, and cholera. In this context, public health departments in the United States proposed extensive cleaning of households, stables, barns, backyards, the use of pesticides, and air purification.[44] A similar deep clean was what ARC humanitarians had in mind for

---

42 Skopje is currently the capital city of the Republic of North Macedonia.
43 Mrs. J.K. Freeman to Colonel H.W. Anderson, "Report on Serbia."
44 Ford, "Bosnia and Herzegovina: Historical Facts."

the people of the Balkans, a practical show-and-tell of what were deemed to be modern hygienic practices.

Besides the targeted attention on epidemics in both curative and preventive terms, the Balkan Commission and local units extended humanitarian work in the medical realm through schemes of infrastructure-building as emergency relief. This was the case in the towns of Gostivar and Prizren in Serbia,[45] which saw the establishment of ad-hoc hospitals, outpatient department care, possibilities to perform surgery, or conditions to address tuberculosis crises in these depleted territories. These were all led by American doctors and nurses, with reportedly collaborative relations with what ARC notes described as "natives." It was also a form of assistance that had provincial undertones, providing services that many people outside Serbia's bigger cities could access. Humanitarians described their work in terms of need in various lands with little to no aid infrastructure, in a region that had seen institutions and regional connections physically destroyed during the war. Importantly, they motivated assistance for people with little possibility to access medical care. In Gostivar, for instance, the dispensary or outpatient department reportedly reached a district containing 6,000 people; furthermore, it transformed this into a central locus of healthcare with people traveling great distances for treatment.[46] In Prizren, a town 60 km off the railroad, ARC was a distribution point for medical supplies, while dispensaries were opened and school children fed.[47]

Second, food relief was another part of ARC's declared emergency humanitarian agenda and effort to alleviate the effects of war in the Balkans. In general, issues of hunger and food scarcity did not represent an overarching dimension of the relief provided by the Balkan Commission after its establishment. This had much to do with the heterogeneity that relief workers observed concerning need in the region; some parts of the Balkans did not see starvation. This was the case in Serbia, where reports noted that food scarcity was not, in fact, an issue.[48] However, in Bosnia and Herzegovina, ARC workers considered it necessary to supplement food intake with an American-type diet, a model of nutrition. There, by 1919, ARC was reportedly supplying milk, sugar, cocoa, and rice, staples of humanitarians' vision of an emergency diet for those suffering from food scarcity.[49]

---

45 Gostivar is currently a town in the Republic of North Macedonia; Prizren is currently a town in Kosovo.
46 Mrs. J.K. Freeman to Colonel H.W. Anderson, "Report on Serbia."
47 Ibid.
48 "What Americans are Doing in the Balkans," Commission to the Balkans, RG 200, Box 893, Records of the American Red Cross, NARA, College Park, MD, USA.
49 Col. Olds Letter to Chief Nurse, "Report on Nursing Situation in the Balkan States."

In Bosnia and Herzegovina, undernourished children received the most attention under the planning of the Balkan Commission. School-age children who were considered emaciated received much of the available food and its provision took place particularly in the school space, an effort that some relief workers considered a step forward in educational practices too. "The attendance of schools has been greatly increased since ARC started giving out breakfast rations," declared one relief worker. To take care of the weak and debilitated children outside schools, ARC established a station at Sarajevo and one at Mostar, where children could receive medical attention and a special ration of food, including soup, rice, and biscuits. In these two cities and at a further fifty-two stations, ARC reported over 10,000 children as recipients of their aid through the establishment of canteens providing an emergency diet. Subsequently, relief reports noted that these canteens became models for the government of the Kingdom of Serbs, Croats, and Slovenes. In humanitarians' understanding, it was through food that these children and these people could really understand the value of the US as their savior through the work of ARC: "American cereal foods had a remarkable fascination for the children who have been accustomed to coarse dishes of corn meal and dry bread. Until the Americans came, 36% of the children lived on bread alone,"[50] noted one relief worker.

Yet, the largest food relief campaign under the aegis of ARC's Balkan Commission took place in Romania, where, according to reports, "an unusual degree of destruction" had taken place during the war.[51] Relief ships with food, alongside clothing and medicine, arrived in Romanian ports immediately after the war. In this context, nationwide food campaigns were organized particularly for widows and orphans, as well as military personnel.[52] Romanians' needs were related to the suffering produced by war, poor harvests, and occupation. But what ARC workers also considered was the potential that the stabilization of these people could lead to: for one worker, this was to save this country from "Bolshevism, revolution, and social disintegration, the evils which accompany the ruin of industry and economic stability."[53] It was also meant to confer opportunities for uncivilized Romanians to observe Americans' "ordinary morality" and "common decency."[54] In this sense, Romanians' deservingness of food relief was not traced merely in terms of suffering and sympathy, but also by the need for their

---

50 Ford, "Bosnia Herzegovina: Historical Facts."
51 "What Americans are Doing in the Balkans."
52 Report of the Balkan Commission in Roumania, Vol.2, 1918–1919, RG 200, Box 893, Records of the American Red Cross, NARA, College Park, MD, USA.
53 Ina B. Rowe, "Historical Narrative of the Balkan Commission of the American Red Cross," RG 200, Box 893, Records of the American Red Cross, NARA, College Park, MD, USA.
54 Report of Galați Unit, Commission to Roumania, 6 March 1919, RG 200, Box 898, Records of the American Red Cross, NARA, College Park, MD, USA.

human nature, alongside society, politics, and the economy to advance and overcome their inherent institutional, but also native backwardness.

Events and effects of war, violence, and destruction created the conjectural impetus for provision of emergency relief by means of medical care and food provision schemes. From this perspective, the Balkans were no different than other sites of humanitarian assistance in this era. However, the practice of ARC's humanitarian aid in the region was also adapted to projections and observations of its disjointed and primitive healthcare infrastructure, lack of institutional organization, and, ultimately, a backwardness that was deemed symptomatic of the long-term presence of Muslim populations. Stabilizing the Balkans, ARC relief workers believed, was to sustain these people from the perspective of survival, but also in terms of political and social equilibrium. However, once the war ended, ARC leadership reconfigured their emergency work also in terms of its reconstructive potential, and the Balkans were to be central to a vision of European rebuilding.

IV. The Allure of Reconstruction: The Case of Orphan Care

The postwar life of ARC was arguably a tumultuous one. The American Relief Administration (ARA), a quasi-governmental organization, largely took the reins of food relief in postwar Europe.[55] With financial support dwindling after the atrocities of the war made the rounds among donors and volunteers, ARC's peacetime work was to be smaller in scope and more intentional. The *need* for emergency relief was also declining, according to humanitarians' assessments. In this context, ideas of a "constructive program" entered the vernacular of ARC humanitarians. This "constructive" dimension of aid meant rehabilitation with long-term effects: humanitarianism was not meant to be a merely urgent band aid, but rather a transformative endeavor according to a new rethinking of ARC-driven assistance.

The Balkans were at the heart of ARC's attraction to reconstruction in Europe, as it echoed missionary work in non-Western societies, where the problematization of civilization and moral backwardness were embedded in the language of aid-giving. In her large exploration of ARC and its work during and after the war, historian Julia Irwin noted that ARC developed its constructive work through an imperial consciousness, as humanitarians sought to intervene in

---

55 For an overview of the various relevant actors of interwar humanitarianism, see Daniel Roger Maul, "The Rise of a Humanitarian Superpower: American NGOs and International Relief, 1917–1945," in *Internationalism Imperialism and the Formation of the Contemporary World: the Pasts of the Present*, edited by Miguel Bandeira Jerónimo and José Pedro Monteiro (London: Palgrave Macmillan, 2018), 127–46.

governance, to eliminate Orientalist tendencies in society and in the political realm, and, ultimately to improve populations and their societies.[56] At the same time, and perhaps rather ironically, they posited their aid as a counter to an Oriental imperial rule that had planted the seeds of backwardness in this region. This was the idea that Henry Anderson, the head of the Balkan Commission, emphasized in a speech regarding ARC's work there when he noted that relief workers must "lay a foundation for a new ideal in their national life" and instill a "sense of obligation and duty which is essential to their own national development, especially in the broad field of international life into which they are now entering." Ultimately, in Anderson's words, ARC's mission was to rebuild the Balkans in a way that would endure long after humanitarians' departure: "The future stability of Europe depends on our ability to establish civilization."[57]

The fate of children in general and orphans in particular emerged as one of the most significant arenas of this constructive humanitarian assistance in this era of the First World War. Orphans were what historian Olivier Faron called the war's "indirect victims,"[58] and saving them, their bodies and their minds, became part of broad visions of state making and nation building in the period. It was an idea that was also at the heart of ARC's new vision of postwar reconstruction in their recipient nations, as orphans, lacking parental guidance, were to be shaped into useful citizens and thus emerge as a civilized generation rather than a lost one. ARC's child relief practices started during the war in France. In that context, the organization interpreted orphans' deservingness of aid through the lens of parentlessness and the weakness of states in caring for their most vulnerable citizens.[59] It was an idea and practice of humanitarian aid that was spread across the continent, from Belgium to Italy to Central and Eastern Europe to the Near East.

For the Balkan Commission too, a viable agenda to encapsulate the vision of rebuilding in the Balkans was child welfare, particularly for orphans. This was to be a commitment that signaled ARC's perception of continuous want in this region and its potency in shaping the next generations and society at large. A report on work in Montenegro written two weeks before the organization's planned exit noted: "The emergency still exists and must be met, but it is possible also to engage in demonstration and educational work which will be of a much

---

56 Irwin, *Making the World Safe*, 158.
57 Henry Anderson, Address to Conference on Situation in the Balkans, 28 May 1919; taken from Irwin, *Making the World Safe*, 158.
58 Olivier Faron, "Aux Côtés, avec, pour les pupilles de la nation. Les forms de mobilization en faveur des orphelins de la Première Guerre mondiale," *Guerres mondiales et conflits contemporains* (2002) 205: 15.
59 Henry P. Davison, *The American Red Cross in the Great War* (New York City, NY: Macmillan, 1919), 165.

more permanent value."⁶⁰ The Montenegro note originally referred to public health assistance, which was to include training of local health officers and nurses, possible establishment of training schools for health purposes, and health demonstrations particularly in rural areas. It was rather an ambitious project that had little feasibility. Indeed, in Montenegro, only a small orphanage existed, whereas the number of orphans was much higher. From some ARC relief workers' perspective, a possible adoption program similar to what had been trialed and tested in Belgium and aid for the expansion of infrastructure for parentless children would signal a commitment to this region's rebuilding.⁶¹

In April 1919, Henry Anderson wrote to Robert Olds, ARC commissioner to Europe, about what the ideal purpose of a child-centric constructive program would entail in Serbia. According to ARC numbers, there were 500,000 orphans in Serbia and in what became the Kingdom of Serbs, Croats, and Slovenes after the Balkan Wars of 1912–1913 and in the aftermath of the First World War. "Something, of course, must be done if these orphans in the next generation are to be benefitted," wrote Anderson, echoing the larger thinking regarding the connections between rebuilding states and nations and orphan care more broadly. In practical terms, ARC workers conceived of a governmental takeover of their initial humanitarian work. At the same time, they envisioned provision of medical care through American doctors and nurses in order to improve orphanages. But Anderson's ambition in making these children useful citizens meshed with the immediacy of postwar life, as he believed that

> "[...] the better children could be taken and placed in industrial schools established by the Government and trained for higher citizenship and possibly a few of the most promising from this school sent to an American college like Cornell, thus leading to the establishment of a better basis suited to Serbian conditions. If we could accomplish this, we might in a very short time change the whole condition of Serbia in the next generation."⁶²

In the following months, ARC established five new orphanages in Serbia, mostly led by Americans but gradually transferred to domestic social workers and local administrators. An envisioned way for orphanage work to further contribute to the making of productive citizens was through the organization of manual training schools that were to sustain a growing working class. Lastly, these Ser-

---

60 H.R. Fairclough, "Comments on the Program for the Balkans Outlined by the Committee," 19 July 1919, Commission to Serbia, Box 904, RG 200, Central File 1917–1934, Records of the American National Red Cross, NARA, College Park, MD., USA.
61 Ibid.
62 Col. Anderson to Robert E. Olds, "Plans for constructive work in Serbia,", 18 April 1919, Commission to Serbia, Box 904, RG 200, Central File 1917–1934, Records of the American National Red Cross, NARA, College Park, MD., USA.

bian children's physical development also mattered, as soup kitchens were maintained at these orphanages, as well as in baby clinics for orphans.[63]

In Romania, ARC declared the special importance of orphan care in the country after the war. Not only were these children parentless, but the more acute scarcity of food in Romania made these children more susceptible to prolonged suffering due to hunger and disease. In this respect, Robert Olds claimed that immediate humanitarian action was needed in the case of these orphans: "Small indeed is the prospect of the child where the only food is cabbage roots or bread made from bran and twigs of trees chopped up together."[64] Addressing health and food crises lay under the umbrella of emergency relief. But Olds believed that this was a way for ARC to have a "broad gauge constructive program, starting in a small way but looking to a larger development"[65] in the case of orphaned children in Romania.

ARC's belief in the more severe plight of orphans in Romania was also indicated by the organization of a special Department of Orphanages in the country. Led by Leonora Lynch, a significant charitable figure in the realm of orphan care in New York, the Department of Orphanages in Romania took over orphans' food relief and launched a campaign to supply local charitable institutions in cities and adjoining territories, a humanitarian effort that was later described as "one of the best records accomplished by any unit in the Commission."[66] Beyond this, the intentional rebuilding of Romania was further situated in planning around orphan care, as education became a form of humanitarian practice. Placing orphaned children in schools and exposing them to (mostly American) culture remained a staple of ARC's constructive work in this region.

These examples of orphan care were not unique instances of orphanage building and ARC assistance across the Balkans. Generally, however, the presence of ARC after 1920 remained deeply limited. The potential for this organization to ensure the "impact" its leaders had envisaged was indirectly proportional to its

---

63 Lena Margaret Johnson to George F. Lyon, "List of Activities of the ARC Commission to Serbia," Commission to Serbia, Box 904, RG 200, Central File 1917–1934, Records of the American National Red Cross, NARA, College Park, MD., USA.
64 E.C. Olds, "The Necessity of Child Relief Work in Roumania," Box 378, Folder 8, Paris Office Countries File 1918–1930, Records of the American Relief Administration European operational records, Reel 446, Microfilms Collection, Hoover Archives Institution, Stanford, CA, USA.
65 "The Future Plan to Roumania," Henry Anderson Letter to Col. Robert E. Olds, 16 July 1919, RG 200, Box 896, Records of the American Red Cross, NARA, College Park, MD, USA.
66 "Report of Activities, Department of Orphanages, Mrs. Leonora A Lynch, Directress," Cpt. H.T. Van Camp Leter to Major L'Engle Hartridge, Bucharest, 26 May 1920, Box 25, Folder 11, Commission to Roumania 1917–1921, Inventory of the American Red Cross records, Reel 36, Microfilms Collection, Hoover Archives Institution, Stanford, CA, USA.

practical abilities, from a financial standpoint, and was also restricted by the paucity of actual workers during a time of declining budgets after the end of the quintessential disaster of the First World War. However, the allure of reconstruction and orphan care as its dimension provide an insight into how ARC workers conceived of the Balkans as a site of intervention with a long-term agenda of stabilization and civilization. Ultimately, the presumption of a backward, but fixable Balkan realm framed the blueprints of ARC's constructive work at large.

V. Conclusion

> "The famine, suffering and misery brought upon this part of Europe by the war have been mitigated in a wonderful degree by the help of the American people through the agency of the Red Cross [...]. Not only have the Americans brought material assistance to these afflicted people, but by their presence they have given them a moral stimulus that will enable them to begin life anew and to provide means in the future of helping themselves and their neighbors."[67]

These were Henry Anderson's words in one of the many reports that ARC humanitarians produced regarding their work in the Balkans. These statements were bold and perhaps exaggerated. However, they were indicative of ways relief workers attached to ARC perceived their mission in the Balkans: teetering between emergency relief to help the sick and the hungry and reconstructive capacities of entire generations of children. Humanitarianism was to feed and cure people in need; but it was also about teaching them how to clean, how to eat, and how to manage their living conditions.

I have argued in this article that humanitarians' perceptions of the Balkans shaped the language and the praxis of aid. They saw this region as one made up of war-torn lands, suppressed by unwanted Oriental imperialism, yet European and vital for the fate of the old continent. In this sense, this article is an analysis and a reflection on the ways Balkanism and humanitarianism intertwined in the era of the First World War. What made the people of the Balkans deserving of humanitarian empathy and action was, in ARC's view, their fundamental suffering, but also their potential for betterment. In narratives of ARC's forays in the region, the people of the Balkans were the uncivilized other, sometimes slow to process humanitarians' modernity. At the same time, reports portrayed their openness to American help. This meshing of perceived insufficiency and potential, of Orientalism and Europeanness, made the Balkans an ideal ground for the expansion – sometimes large, sometimes patchy – of ARC's reconstructive humanitarianism in the era of the First World War.

---

67 "What Americans are Doing in the Balkans."

Katharina Seibert

Springboards for Women's Careers. International Humanitarianism, the Spanish Civil War, and the Rise of Mercedes Milá Nolla

I. Mercedes Milá – a Case Study for Female Careers in Humanitarianism

"I founded the Damas de Sanidad Militar, thanks to the studies I had done here in Spain and in England through the Red Cross. General Franco appointed me Inspector General of all the Female Services in the military hospitals in March 1937. I had to organize everything, the nurses had to be given courses […] Even at the front, during the breaks in the fighting, doctors and nurses gave classes. So, when the war was over, these nurses knew a lot."[1]

Interviewed in old age, Mercedes Milá Nolla proudly looked back on her work as a nurse during the Spanish Civil War. In Spain's history of war nursing, Mercedes Milá stood out not only because she belonged to the small group of the best-trained nurses in the country at the time, but because she was the founding mother of the nurses' corps of the Francoist armed forces and thus the first woman to officially become part of Franco's army during the Civil War (1936–1939/48).[2] Mercedes Milá was a representative of the women of Spain's so-called "traditional elites," who sided with Franco and thus helped build his dictatorship. She was also a representative of upper-class women who found in humanitarian organizations and relief work an opportunity to build independent careers for themselves. She is the protagonist of this paper, and her story serves as a case

---

I thank Anca Cretu and Julia Schulte-Werning! It was a pleasure working with you on this special issue. Thank you also to the editorial board of Zeitgeschichte. And finally, thank you Sarah, for your feedback and thoughts while developing my paper, and for the wonderful cooperation we had while putting this issue together.

1 All translations from Spanish to English are mine and edited by John Heath. Concha Gómez, Mercedes Milá: "La enfermera más anciana de la Institución", in: *Cruz Roja*, 856, September–October 1984, 44–47, cit. Josep Carles Clemente, *La Escuela Universitaria de Enfermeras de Madrid. Historia de una iniciativa humanitaria de la Cruz Roja Española (1918–1997)*, (Madrid: Fundamentos Colección Ciencia, 1999), 275.
2 Nicholas Coni, "The Head of All the Nurses," *International Journal of Iberian Studies*, 22 (2009) 1: 79–84, 81–82.

study with which to approach the question as to how humanitarianism, civil war, and female career building intersected in Spain during its fundamental political transformation from the end of the Restoration system to the Second Republic and early Francoism.

Mercedes Milá's life trajectory also includes a crucial moment in the history of humanitarianism. As Rebecca Gill emphasizes, "the field of relief work emerged in close […] connection with the professionalization of nursing, as well as army reform."[3] The rise of the secular nurse in Spain as a feminimized profession was propelled by the Spanish Civil War. At the same time, this process took place against the backdrop of the Great War and its (long-term) effects. It received a tailwind from these transformations. On the international level of humanitarianism and philanthropy, the Great War changed the perception of humanitarians on their missions. The gradual emergence of an "unsatiable humanitarian market"[4] went hand in hand with processes of standardization and differentiation of relief work into various (gendered) professions, logistics, and planification – "organized giving,"[5] as Norbert Götz, Georgina Brewis, and Steffen Werther call it. In the wake of these transformations, women gained more importance as relief workers. However, as Dolores Martín Moruno, Brenda Lynn Edgar, and Marie Leyder rightly point out, at the same time, this expansion of feminimized professions in humanitarianism came with a glass ceiling. Even today, women only seldomly occupy management positions in international humanitarian organizations, although they are sought after as a labor force.[6] In other words, while humanitarianism started to systematically embrace women as humanitarian workers, they were also systematically relegated to subordinate positions.

When we look at women like Mercedes Milá, however, stories come to the fore that the historiography of humanitarianism has still largely neglected. Her biography shows that the world of humanitarian philanthropy offered her an opportunity to start a career in healthcare and war relief work, but that she also appropriated these learnings in a way that enabled her to take her career to the next level within the political project of Francoist state-building. While she started her vocational training as a nurse in courses offered by the Spanish

---

3 Rebecca Gill, *Calculating Compassion: Humanity and Relief in War, Britain 1870–1914* (Manchester: Manchester University Press 2016), 18.
4 Norbert Götz/Georgina Brewis/Steffen Werther, "Humanitäre Hilfe. Eine Braudel'sche Perspektive", in: *Freiwilligenarbeit und gemeinnützige Organisationen im Wandel*, ed. by Nicole Kramer, Christine G. Krüger, Historische Zeitschrift/Beihefte 76, (Berlin/Boston: De Gruyter 2019), 89–120, 95.
5 Ibid., 96.
6 Dolores Martín-Moruno/Brenda Lynn Edgar/Marie Leyder, "Feminist Perspectives on the History of Humanitarian Relief (1870–1945)," *Medicine, Conflict and Survival*, 36 (2020) 1: 2–18, 4.

Committee of the Red Cross (SRC) and used the international networks the Red Cross Movement offered her, she later decided to leave the so-called impartial world of humanitarianism behind and to join Franco. Appointed inspector general of all the Female Services in the Health Service (SFSM[7]) in 1937, she achieved a position of far-reaching decision-making power in the dawning dictatorship. International humanitarianism provided her thus a springboard to building a career in Spain. These entanglements of national and international developments are at the heart of this paper.

Taking her professional career as a case study[8] means pointing out the exceptionalities of her trajectory, but also analyzing larger structures that enabled women like her to gain access to medical and humanitarian careers. Case studies provide an opportunity to take up "the issues of singularity and generalization in a productive way,"[9] as Johanna Gehmacher maintains. "A case, therefore, is neither merely an example of something already sufficiently known, nor a singular and incomparable event. [...] the case never stands for itself; it always formulates a question within a larger context and is therefore a means to an end,"[10] as Gehmacher further argues. From the perspective of the history of humanitarianism, zooming in on Mercedes Milá and her professional biography offers insight into how actors of medical relief work navigated, in their day-to-day lives and their careers, the blurred lines between transnational philanthropy, international knowledge production and standardization, and national domestic but also international politics.

International humanitarian organizations provided the networks for knowledge exchange and standardization in medical humanitarianism and scientific philanthropy. Organizations like the Red Cross, the Rockefeller Foundation, or the League of Nations Health Organization left deep traces in the configurations of national training programs and research thanks to their efforts to cultivate expert knowledge and circulation.[11] At the same time, as "floating"[12] institutions,

---

7 I will use the abbreviation of the Spanish term as reference throughout this text: Servicios Femeninos de Sanidad Militar (SFSM).
8 Johanna Gehmacher, "A Case for Female Individuality: Käthe Schirmacher – Self-Invention and Biography," in *Case Studies and the Dissemination of Knowledge*, ed. by Joy Damousi, Birgit Lang, and Katie Sutton (New York: Routledge, 2015), 66–81; John Cash, "The Case Study as Representative Anecdote," in *Case Studies and the Dissemination of Knowledge*, ed. by Joy Damousi, Birgit Lang, and Katie Sutton (New York: Routledge, 2015), 31–48.
9 Gehmacher, "A Case for Female Individuality," 68.
10 Ibid.
11 John Farley, "The International Health Division of the Rockefeller Foundation: the Russell Years, 1920–1934," in *International Health Organisations and Movements, 1918–1939* ed. by Paul Weindling, (Cambridge: Cambridge University Press, 1995), 203–221; Iris Borowy, *Coming to Terms with World Health: the League of Nations Health Organisation 1921–1946*, (Frankfurt am Main; New York: Peter Lang, 2009); Josep Lluís Barona Vilar, *Health Policies in*

humanitarian organizations had to constantly negotiate with governments and local stakeholders to secure their projects and own interests. But they also had to deal with the fact that their relief workers changed careers and affiliations, had their own agendas and goals, and had to juggle the expectations of the different roles they held in their societies.

During the interwar period, humanitarianism in Spain was an elitist project that attracted primarily members of the social upper classes. How class, gender, and political affiliation mattered are therefore key questions I address in my intersectional analysis. Drawing predominantly on Mercedes Milá's vast correspondence from her time as inspector general, an interview, and additional sources, the paper primarily focuses on Mercedes Milá as an historical actor. Her perspective guides the analysis, which raises three questions: how did international humanitarianism become her springboard to a career in Francoist Spain? How did the Civil War as a domestic event become an opportunity to briefly break the glass ceiling for female relief professionals? And how did transnational humanitarianism prevail in early Francoism?

II. A Classist Project: Becoming a Professional Nurse

Mercedes Milá was among the first generation of women who were trained to become professional bedside nurses outside monastery walls. This generation of healthcare workers was in some respects a homogenous social group, as they all belonged to the social middle and upper classes, who could afford and supported higher education for their daughters. The institutions that first took the opportunity and offered standardized nursing trainings defined admission criteria that intensified this class effect. The Spanish Committee of the Red Cross played a key role in this process. Until the formal secularization of bedside nursing in 1915,[13] the SRC was the most prominent organization that offered women the opportunity to engage in humanitarian work. However, from its foundation, the SRC attracted and recruited predominantly members of the upper social classes

---

Interwar Europe: A Transnational Perspective, Routledge Studies in the History of Science, Technology and Medicine 34 (Abingdon, Oxon; New York, NY: Routledge, 2019).

12 Joël Glasman, "Die Politik aus dem Nirgendwo. Humanitäre Hilfe und die Geschichte schwereloser Institutionen," *Geschichte der Gegenwart*, November 27, 2022: https://geschichtedergegenwart.ch/die-politik-aus-dem-nirgendwo-humanitaere-hilfe-und-die-geschichte-schwereloser-institutionen/ last access: February 10, 2024.

13 María López Vallecillo, *Presencia social e imagen pública de las enfermeras en el siglo XX (1915–1940)*, Ph.D. Thesis, (Universidad de Valladolid 2016), 35–36.

and did not necessarily seek to include women of a lower social standing.[14] Even though, it was humanitarian organizations such as the SRC that provided access to women to medical and healthcare knowledge and opened the doors for them to build a career. In these early days of bedside nursing as a secular profession, becoming a nurse was nevertheless a classist project and Mercedes Milá was the perfect candidate.

She was born in Barcelona on 22 September 1895 to a senior naval officer in Ceuta who served on hospital ships.[15] She was also the niece of wealthy Barcelonese industrialists.[16] Later her family moved to Madrid, where she attended a Catholic convent school. During her schooling she spent a year abroad in England and learned English.[17] Mercedes Milá and her family belonged to what historiography refers to as the "traditional" elites, meaning the affluent upper-middle and upper classes in Spain, which predominantly consisted of the members of the Spanish nobility, large landowning families, wealthy industrialists, and the army. These social groups were, furthermore, often closely connected with the Spanish Catholic Church, another very influential actor in Spanish society at the turn of the century and beyond. These so-called traditional elites can be understood as the social groups that had accumulated for generations and solidified their significant economic and political power throughout the 19th century. In other words, Mercedes Milá was a member of a wealthy and very well-connected family that was capable of opening many doors for her and supported her in furthering her education.

"I started very young. When I became a Dama de la Cruz Roja, I was 22 years old,"[18] Mercedes Milá mentioned in an interview with Concha Gómez for the journal of the Red Cross in 1984. When asked why she chose nursing for her vocational training, she answered, "If I went into nursing, I could accompany my father."[19] This statement mirrors an observation historian Jon Arrizabalaga stressed in his works. He explains that in the late 19th and early 20th century it was a common practice for daughters or wives to join the SRC to be closer to their husbands or fathers, especially when if they were military doctors or army officials. That way, medicine, the SRC, and the social upper classes became in-

---

14 On the history of the first women's groups in the SRC, see inter alia Jon Arrizabalaga, "The 'Merciful and Loving Sex': Concepción Arenal's Narratives on Spanish Red Cross Women's War Relief Work in the 1870s," *Medicine, Conflict and Survival*, 36 (2020) 1: 41–60.
15 Fundación Nacional Francisco Franco, "Mercedes Milá Nolla, la abnegación," 03.02.2013, https://fnff.es/memoria-historica/mercedes-mila-nolla-la-abnegacion/ last access: February 29, 2024.
16 Pere Milà i Camps and Roser Segmon i Artells, they are famous for their Gaudí-built house "Casa Milá," also known as "La Pedrera" in Barcelona.
17 Coni, "The Head of All the Nurses", 80.
18 Gómez, Mercedes Milá, cit. Clemente, *La Escuela Universitaria*, 273.
19 Ibid.

timately entangled. In other words, classism and elite networks became the backbone of early humanitarianism in Spain. This development was not, however, peculiar to Spain. As Matthias Schulz argues, in many other European countries the founders of national Red Cross Committees actively sought and entertained close connections with the political elite of their country. Royal endorsement, for instance, was seen as a helpful tool for rooting humanitarian philanthropy institutionally.[20] It was the same in Spain. The founders of the Spanish Section of the Red Cross were themselves aristocrats and involved with the Ministry of War. They used their connections to the army, the upper social classes, and the Catholic Church to root the new humanitarian organization in Spanish society.[21] The first women's section of the SRC reflects this development, too, which was particularly relevant for Mercedes Milá starting her career. The first women's groups of the SRC were founded by a group of philanthropic aristocratic women[22] and Queen Victoria Eugenia de Battenberg became the institution's patroness (1906–1931).[23] Mercedes Milá obviously understood how Spanish humanitarianism worked because when she decided to become a nurse, she personally wrote a letter to the queen.[24] It speaks to the social status she and her family enjoyed that she received a positive response.

Mercedes Milá began her vocational training as a *Dama Enfermera*[25] in 1917 against the backdrop of the Great War, when, for the first time, masses of women were recruited as war nurses to tend to the armies' casualties. After the war was over, the long-term effects of the war put into question humanitarian relief work as a measure to humanize warfare and its limitation to wartime. This put the role of women as relief workers on the agendas of NGOs and international organizations such as the International Committee of the Red Cross (ICRC), the re-

---

20 Matthias Schulz, "Dilemmas of "Geneva" Humanitarian Internationalism: The International Committee of the Red Cross and the Red Cross Movement, 1863–1918," in *Dilemmas of Humanitarian Aid in the Twentieth Century* ed. by Johannes Paulmann, Studies of the German Historical Institute London, (Oxford: Oxford University Press, 2016), 35–62, 44–45.
21 Jon Arrizabalaga and Juan Carlos García Reyes, "Between a Humanitarian Ethos and the Military Efficiency: The Early Days of the Spanish Red Cross, 1864–1876," in *Schlachtschrecken – Konventionen. Das Rote Kreuz und die Erfindung der Menschlichkeit im Kriege* ed. by Wolfgang U. Eckart, Philipp Osten, (Herbolzheim: Centaurus Verlag & Media, 2011), 49–65.
22 Arrizabalaga, "The 'Merciful and Loving Sex,'" 43–44.
23 Clemente, La Escuela Universitaria, 32–34.
24 Gómez, Mercedes Milá, cit. at Clemente, *La Escuela Universitaria*, 273.
25 The SRC offered a two-tier programme. The first addressed upper-class women who wanted to professionalize in medical charity work (Damas Enfermeras). See María López Vallecillo, *Enfermeras: Mujeres protagonistas en los conflictos bélicos de la primera mitad del siglo XX en España* (Pamplona: EUNSA, 2021), 21–44.

cently founded League of Red Cross Societies (LORCS),[26] and the Rockefeller Foundation.[27] In this context, public health emerged as a professional field that was quickly femininized and subordinated to medicine. These international developments helped define new standards in humanitarian relief work, which also affected medical care work in more general terms. Through the networks of the Red Cross movement, these bodies of knowledge were received by the SRC, too, and influenced the efforts of the SRC – and of other Spanish medical and healthcare institutions[28] that were also in the process of setting up nursing programs.

"We were few," recalled Mercedes Milá, also stating that the training was "very serious" and "strict."[29] One of the reasons for that may have been that the admission criteria favored particularly well-connected upper-middle and upper-class women with a medical family background. According to María López Vallecillo, to be elected for the training as a *Dama Enfermera* a woman had to be at least seventeen years old and already a member of the Red Cross, prove her physical fitness, provide a letter of endorsement from two members of the SRC, accept the regulations and norms, and prove sufficient school education.[30] In her formation at the SRC, Mercedes Milá studied theoretical-medical knowledge and learned practical skills of bedside nursing. The training format for a *Dama Enfermera* was a two-tier system. The first course was short and took only a few months, while the second meant studying theory for a year and then six months of practical training.[31] The first training track for *Damas Enfermeras* was attended predominantly by women who wanted to do charity work, while the second course enabled its students to actually learn the craft of bedside nursing. Mercedes Milá did both courses and graduated in 1921.[32]

For Mercedes Milá, the Red Cross was both the first step to becoming a professional nurse and the context in which she first came into contact with the international scientific networks of medical and nursing knowledge production and circulation. In her interview with Concha Gómez, she mentioned that she was trained by a French and a British nun-nurse, whom she described as very thor-

---

26 Melanie Oppenheimer, "Nurses of the League: The League of Red Cross Societies and the Development of Public Health Nursing Post-WWI," *History Australia*, 17 (2020) 4: 628–644.
27 Anne-Emanuelle Birn and Elizabeth Fee, "The Art of Medicine. The Rockefeller Foundation and the International Health Agenda," *The Lancet*, 381 (2013) May 11: 1618–1619.
28 Fernando Salmón Muñiz, Jon Arrizabalaga, and Luis García Ballester, "La introducción del hospital contemporáneo en España: La quiebra del modelo originario de organización de la Casa de Salud Valdecilla de Santander" *Dynamis, Acta Hispanica ad Medicinae Scientiariiumque Historiam Illustrandam*, 7–8 (1987): 249–273.
29 Gómez, Mercedes Milá, cit. at Clemente, *La Escuela Universitaria*, 274.
30 López Vallecillo, *Enfermeras*, 25.
31 Ibid., 26–27.
32 Fundación Nacional Francisco Franco, Mercedes Milá Nolla.

ough and good. Apparently, these two nuns were invited to come to Spain because it was the queen's express ambition to shape the newly established SRC nursing programs according to the international standards of the time.[33] The involvement of Spain's aristocracy paid off, as they provided the network and the means to invest in then modern nursing training. The second step towards this world of academicized medicine and nursing was taken by Mercedes Milá a few years after she graduated. She was selected to study Public Health in the class of 1926/27 at Bedford College, London.[34] This program was a joint venture of Bedford College, the LORCS, and the Rockefeller Foundation.[35] From the launch of the first hygiene course in 1896, the all-women's Bedford College, became a hotspot in European academia for women who wanted to study public health, hygiene, and social work.[36] "My parents let me go and so I went,"[37] she said of this next phase of her formal training. Nicholas Coni relates that she was "regarded as very able and emerged with a first-class diploma (Royal Holloway 1926–1927)."[38]

In London, Mercedes Milá stepped into the pluralizing world of "professional humanitarianism"[39] and "scientific philanthropy."[40] This world of experts and professionals was strongly influenced by the new constellation of international organizations and NGOs which had emerged in the aftermath of the Great War and which defined and competed for a place in the world of humanitarianism. Historiography on these organizations further emphasizes that they not only contributed to cultivating expert knowledge but also invested in team building efforts among their fellows and functionaries. That way, powerful transnational networks formed.[41] At Bedford College, Mercedes Milá received the opportunity

---

33 Gómez, Mercedes Milá, cit. at Clemente, *La Escuela Universitaria*, 274.
34 Coni, "The Head of All the Nurses," 80.
35 Royal Holloway Archives and Special Collections, University of London, Bedford College Papers. Administrative / Biographical History.
36 Linna Bentley and Bedford College (eds.), Educating Women: A Pictorial History of Bedford College, University of London, 1849–1985, Surrey 1991, 3, 22–23.
37 Gómez, Mercedes Milá, cit. at Clemente, *La Escuela Universitaria*, 274.
38 Coni, "The Head of All the Nurses", 80.
39 Johannes Paulmann, "The Dilemmas of Humanitarian Aid: Historical Perspectives", in *Dilemmas of Humanitarian Aid in the Twentieth Century* ed. by Johannes Paulmann, Studies of the German Historical Institute London, (Oxford: Oxford University Press, 2016), 1–31, 14; Silvia Salvatici, *A History of Humanitarianism, 1755–1989: In the Name of Others*, Humanitarianism, (Manchester: Manchester University Press, 2019), 51–52, 80–83; Anthony Redmond, "Professionalisation of the Humanitarian Response", in *The Routledge Companion to Humanitarian Action*, ed. by Roger Mac Ginty, Jenny H. Peterson, (Abdingdon, Ox: Routledge 2015), 403–416.
40 Birn/Fee, "The Art of Medicine," 1618–1619.
41 Birn/Fee, "The Art of Medicine."; Iris Borowy, Anne Hardy (eds.), *Of Medicine and Men: Biographies and Ideas in European Social Medicine Between the World Wars*, (Frankfurt am Main; New York: Peter Lang, 2008), 9–11.

not only to study then cutting-edge nursing and public health knowledge, but also to expand her professional networks beyond the borders of Spain.

Mercedes Milá's stay in London was not only about studying new theories on public health and nursing and learning new skills. She also learned much about how nursing could be organized. "There [at Bedford College, K. S.] I learned that the nurses of other countries like France, Canada, Austria, etc. were all trained as First-Class Professional Nurses, these people held leading positions [in the hospitals, K. S.]. The only one who was not a professional, was me."[42] Mercedes Milá's encounter with her fellow students in London and the influences of international humanitarian organizations convinced her that care work in a modern healthcare system had to be coordinated by women who were trained to international standards. This realization stood in sharp contrast to the status quo in Spain.[43] As a *Dama Enfermera* she was well appreciated but hospital hierarchies were still predominantly governed by men and nuns. It was therefore the encounter and comparison with other European countries that led Mercedes Milá to also question the organizational structure of the healthcare system in place in Spain.

Over the course of the following years, she successfully made a name for herself as a qualified and able nurse. In 1934, she took the next step in her career when she accepted the government's offer to set up Spain's first school for public health (Escuela de Enfermeras Visitadoras Sanitarias).[44] Looking back on her life, she maintained, "I introduced the reform in nursing"[45] in Spain. While Josep Bernabeu Mestre and Encarna Gascón Pérez confirm that Mercedes Milá did play a central role in modernizing the nursing profession after the Civil War was over, of course, there were others involved, too.[46]

The SRC not only provided Mercedes Milá with access to a career in nursing and international networks. It also offered her the opportunity to gather firsthand experiences in war nursing, which was important for her next crucial career step. During the Rif War (1921-1926) she was deployed to Morocco as a war nurse with the SRC.[47] Along with a group of SRC nurses, she was sent to Melilla, where

---

42 Ibid.
43 Anna Ramió et al. focused on Catalunya. Considering that Catalunya was the most progressive region in Spain regarding secularization during the 1920s and 1930s, their findings can be assumed to be relevant for the whole territory of Spain. Ramió/Torres (eds.), *Enfermeras de guerra*, 33-34.
44 Josep Bernabeu Mestre, Encarnación Gascón Pérez, *Historia de la enfermería de salud pública en España: (1860-1977)*, (Alicante: Universidad de Alicante, 1999), 93-94.
45 Gómez, Mercedes Milá, cit. at Clemente, *La Escuela Universitaria*, 276.
46 Bernabeu Mestre/Gascón Pérez, *Historia de la enfermería de salud pública en España*, 102-108, 112-127.
47 Nicholas Coni, *Medicine and Warfare: Spain, 1936-1939*, Cañada Blanch Studies on Contemporary Spain 16, (New York: Routledge 2007), 30.

they helped to set up hospitals, sickbays, and milk feeding stations. Eventually, they also worked as nurses and engaged with fundraising. They organized, for instance, donations for the "aguinaldo del soldado" – the soldiers' Christmas bonus.[48] It was on Moroccan soil that Mercedes Milá gathered important experiences of how healthcare logistics worked in the military context during a war. In this way she learned how to cooperate with military officials, how to organize the day-to-day running of a military hospital, and much more. All of this knowledge and the international networks came in handy when she decided to become a Francoist nurse during the Civil War.

During the first twenty years of her career, the SRC and international humanitarianism enabled Mercedes Milá to form her professional identity as a modern nurse – "modern" according to the international state of the art at the time. Against the background of interwar humanitarianism and medicine, she built an impressive career and became an influential and well-trained nurse in Spain. Until the Civil War began, she was, however, in good company. Although they were still few in number, during the 1920s and 1930s Spain saw the rise of a first generation of women as medical workers, some of whom became nurses like Teresa Junquera Ibrán,[49] while others studied medicine like Ampara Poch y Gascón.[50]

III. A Political Decision: Becoming a Francoist Nurse

Mercedes Milá's career in nursing took place against the backdrop of fundamental political change on the international level, but also in Spain. When she signed up for the *Dama Enfermera* course in 1917, Spain was still a constitutional monarchy under King Alfonso XIII (1886–1931). When she left the country to study in London, Spain was still officially a monarchy but by then governed by the military dictator Miguel Primo de Rivera (1923–1930). When she was already established as an expert in public health and nursing, the Restoration system failed at the ballot box on 14 April 1931, and subsequently the Second Republic (1931–1939) was proclaimed. When the Civil War began in 1936 and the Spanish society was forced to take sides, she was caught in the middle. By then, everything had become politicized, even nursing. Under these circumstances, Mercedes Milá took a political decision and started the next important step in her career. She

---

48 Francisco Javier Martínez, "Estado de necesidad. La Cruz Roja Española en Marruecos", 1886–1927, *História, Ciências, Saúde – Manguinhos*, 23 (2016) 3: 867–886, 875–876.
49 Salmón Muñiz/Arrizabalaga/García Ballester, "La introducción del hospital contemporáneo en España", 269–270.
50 Antonina Rodrigo, *Una mujer libre: Amparo Poch y Gascón: médica anarquista*, Colección Tramontana 6, (Barcelona 2002).

became a Francoist nurse. When the war began, however, a nurses' corps did not yet exist in the Francoist army. It had yet to be founded. Therefore, becoming a Francoist nurse entailed the interplay of different developments in the arena of medical humanitarianism and war relief work, Civil War, and the building of the Francoist dictatorship.

On 17 July 1936, a junta of military generals staged a coup d'état but failed, and thus the Civil War began. Two months later, Francisco Franco assumed power over the putschist armed forces and the insurgent territories. Spain's history of almost forty years of Francoist dictatorship began. Violence and casualty numbers quickly rose thanks to the early frontline combat and the terror in the rearguard and on the home front, causing great demand for medical attention and humanitarian relief work. In places like Pamplona, Burgos, or Salamanca, the coup d'état was greeted frenetically by the civilian population, whereas in places like Madrid, Barcelona, and Bilbao, people took to the streets to defend the Second Republic. Along the political divide between left and right, Spain fell apart into two warring zones. The socio-political division was marked by class biases as the working class rose to defend the Second Republic and many parts of the affluent upper classes sided with the putschists. Importantly, this schism affected the field of healthcare, providing actors and humanitarian organizations which were dominated by members of the upper classes.

Mercedes Milá was in Madrid when the coup failed, and thus on Republican territory. The resistance of Madrilenians and the remaining police forces to the military insurrection in Madrid is still legendary today.[51] While the government shuffled and hesitated to arm the people, trade unions and leftist militia together with loyal security forces responded to the coup d'état and successfully prevented the soldiers from leaving the garrison and taking over the government.[52] In time, Madrid became the beating heart of the Republic. Particularly during the first weeks and months of the war, the city was controlled and governed by leftist organizations. A mixture of social revolution and militia-controlled police forces searching the city for potential enemy subversion turned Madrid into a place where the affluent upper classes, representatives of right-wing or rightist politics, and anyone who was considered an opponent to social revolution faced repression.[53] According to Nicholas Coni, Mercedes Milá initially set up a military

---

51 Fernando Jiménez Herrera, "El golpe fracasa, la revolución toma las calles. Los comités revolucionarios (verano-otoño de 1936)", in *Asedio: historia de Madrid en el Guerra Civil (1936-1939)*, ed. by Gutmaro Gómez Bravo, Serie Investigación 13, (Madrid: Ediciones Complutense 2018), 321-351, 321-322; Santos Juliá, *Hoy no es ayer: ensayos sobre la España del siglo XX*, Temas de Actualidad, (Barcelona: RBA 2010), 64-65.
52 Julián Casanova, *The Spanish Republic and Civil War*, (Cambridge; New York 2010), 153.
53 Fernando Jiménez Herrera, *El mito de las checas: historia y memoria de los comités revolucionarios (Madrid, 1936)*, (Granada: Comares Historia 2021), 54-91.

hospital in the Hotel Ritz in Madrid during the first days of the war but eventually fled the city.[54] As an upper class Catholic woman with an industrialist family background and army ties, she belonged to the social groups that defenders of the Second Republic suspected of being hostile to the working classes. According to the Fundación Nacional Francisco Franco, Mercedes Milá's contacts in the Red Cross in Geneva helped her to leave the country and to enter Francoist Spain.[55] Leaving Madrid and renouncing the Republic was her first step towards becoming a Francoist nurse. The next step, however, was out of her control, because the formation of a Francoist nurses' corps depended on developments that unfolded on the streets and on the frontlines and set humanitarianism and medical assistance in motion.

Parallel to Mercedes Milá's departure from Madrid, the SRC was dissolved. According to Gabriel Pretus, on 20 July 1936 militia units entered the SRC headquarters and forced the SRC president, General Ricardo Berruguete y Lana, to dismiss his staff and resign. Most of the SRC staff were replaced by politically "trustworthy" medical personnel.[56] The pediatrician Aurelio Romeo Lozano was made the new president of the Republican Red Cross Committee. At the same time, another Committee of the Spanish Red Cross was founded in putschist Burgos under the leadership of Fernando Suárez de Tangil, count of Vallellano. These events worried the Geneva headquarters and a few days later, the ICRC sent Swiss doctor Marcel Junod to negotiate an agreement with both warring parties. The ICRC feared a humanitarian catastrophe was looming and was eager to organize its own humanitarian intervention in Spain.[57] According to Alfonso García López, the creation of two committees caused serious diplomatic controversy among international humanitarians, the Republican government claiming that the recognition of the Francoist Red Cross internationally delegitimized their status as a democratically elected government of Spain.[58] The ICRC delegate eventually managed to negotiate the co-existence of two Spanish Red Cross Committees which agreed to work under the imperative of impartiality.

The foundation of two Red Cross Committees with all related controversies and problems affected the healthcare systems of both warring factions.[59] In the

---

54 Coni, "The Head of All the Nurses", 80.
55 Fundación Nacional Francisco Franco, Mercedes Milá Nolla.
56 Gabriel Pretus, *La ayuda humanitaria en la guerra civil española: 1936–1939*, (Albolote, Granada: Comares Historia 2015), 45.
57 Ibid., 46.
58 Alfonso García López, *Entre el odio y la venganza: El CICR en la Guerra Civil española*, (La Coruña: Espacio Cultura 2016), 22–23.
59 Some insight on the Republican side offer among others, Xavier García Ferrandis, "La asistencia sanitaria en la Provincia de Valencia durante la Guerra Civil Española (1936–1939)" *Llull, Revista de la Sociedad Española de Historia de las Ciencias y de las Técnicas*, 34 (2011)

case of Francoist Spain, the re-organization of the Francoist Red Cross meant that the institution was partially paralyzed, since large parts of their infrastructure remained on Republican territory. At the same time, many of the prewar SRC members sided with the insurgent generals. A network of well-versed Red Cross workers thus ended up in the Francoist zone. For Mercedes Milá this meant that many of her former fellow *Damas Enfermeras* and acquaintances of the SRC joined the Francoists and started to rebuild the organization.

These events also enabled other healthcare actors to step in. While Mercedes Milá was fleeing Republican Spain and SRC was under reconstruction, the demand for medical humanitarianism and relief workers grew quickly in the Francoist zones. As part of the popular response, people were mobilized for tasks supporting the war effort, such as healthcare and relief work. Among these efforts, some women's organizations on the Francoist side stood out, namely the female section of fascist Falange, the Sección Femenina, which was founded only in 1934 but quickly began to rally new members,[60] but also the ultra-Catholic, reactionary, monarchist Carlist Margaritas, and some Catholic women's organizations like Acción Católica de la Mujer, an experienced actor of female mobilization.[61] All of them instantly called up women to support them in collecting donations, food, and clothes for the fighting units; they set up canteens for orphaned or neglected children, but they also organized crash courses in first aid measures and nursing basics.[62] In other words, they engaged in humanitarian tasks. According to María López Vallecillo, the emergence of such initiatives was comparable to mushrooms sprouting all over insurgent territory.[63] Many of these women were engaged in rearguard relief work, while others volunteered in military hospitals. In addition, these organizations set up their relief work projects, such as the Falangist Auxilio Social[64] or the Carlist Frentes y Hospitales.

73, 1: 13–38; Josep Lluís Barona, Josep Bernabeu Mestre, *La salud y el estado: el movimiento sanitario internacional y la administración española (1815–1945)*, Oberta Història 144, (Valencia 2008).

60 Toni Morant i Ariño, "'Las mujeres que también fueron fascistas.' Los primeros años de la Sección Femenina de Falange en una mirada transnacional" *Historia del Presente*, (2018) 32, 11–26; Inbal Ofer, "A 'New' Woman for a 'New' Spain: The Sección Femenina de la Falange and the Image of the National Syndicalist Woman", *European History Quarterly*, 39 (2009) 4: 583–605.

61 Inmaculada Blasco Herranz, "Citizenship and Female Catholic Militancy in 1920s Spain", *Gender & History*, 19 (2007) 3: 441–466; Antonio Manuel Moral Roncal, "María Rosa Urraca Pastor: De la militancia en Acción Católica a la palestra política carlista (1900–1936)", *Historia y Política*, 26 (2011): 199–226.

62 María López Vallecillo, "Relevancia de la mujer en el bando nacional de la Guerra Civil española: las enfermeras", *Memoria y Civilización*, 19 (2016), 419–439.

63 Ibid., 421–422.

64 Ángela Cenarro Lagunas, "El Auxilio Social de Falange (1936–1940): Entre la guerra total y el 'Nuevo Estado' franquista", *Bulletin of Spanish Studies*, 91 (2014) 1-2: 43–59; María del

In other words, the coup and the subsequent reorganization of the Red Cross caused a shift in power relations among humanitarian organizations, allowing for new actors to enter the stage of humanitarian relief work.

During the initial stages of the war, the key cities for pharmaceutical production, storage, and hospital infrastructure remained in the Republican zone.[65] The civilian medical infrastructure in general was overwhelmed on both sides, as were the army Health Services. In the Francoist zones, initiatives like the Sección Femenina's and Margaritas' were welcomed. Even though large parts of the prewar Health Service staff sided with the coup, the army health infrastructure was underequipped and understaffed for a "total war."[66] The recruitment of doctors and nursing staff overwhelmed the drafting bureaus.[67] With the Red Cross in disarray and the army Health Service in the process of adapting to mass warfare, in many places the fighting units depended on the support of the local population. A frontline surgeon recalled, "[d]uring the first weeks of the war we received masses of casualties. [...] They came in in horrible conditions."[68] "'There won't be no youth left when this is over' we told each other,"[69] a Margarita recalled conversations with her colleagues at a field hospital during the summer of 1936. Volunteers with and without medical skills were recruited to fill the gaps in military healthcare. This ad hoc and random recruitment produced ambivalent results, as the following report of winter 1936/37 showcases:

> "But in those localities where neither medical schools nor local Red Cross committees can train nurses, they have had to accept [...] female staff, who lack in any training and rely solely on their goodwill to help the nuns, who, due to their small numbers, are burdened with a truly overwhelming workload. There are hospitals in which [...] female staff [...] are tolerated by doctors and nuns [...]; in other establishments they are scarce because there are doctors who treat them with hostility because they disturb the stillness, calm, and silence necessary for the patients [...]; the same happens with the nuns, who not always accept the presence of this staff."[70]

Carmen Giménez Muñoz, "La asistencia social en Sevilla: Del Auxilio de Invierno al Auxilio Social (1936–1939)," *HISPANIA NOVA. Revista de Historia Contemporánea*, 9 (2009): 1–37; Mónica Orduña Prada, *El Auxilio Social (1936–1940): la etapa fundacional y los primeros años*, (Madrid 1996).

65 Coni, *Medicine and Warfare*, 23.
66 Roger Chickering, "The Spanish Civil War in the Age of Total War", in *"If you tolerate this..." The Spanish Civil War in the Age of Total War* ed. by Martin Baumeister and Stefanie Schüler-Springorum (Frankfurt a. M.: Campus, 2008), 28–46.
67 James Matthews, *Reluctant Warriors: Republican Popular Army and Nationalist Army Conscripts in the Spanish Civil War, 1936–1939*, (Oxford: Oxford University Press 2012), 2–3.
68 Ibid., 433.
69 Ibid., 762.
70 Cuartel General del Generalísimo, Estado Mayor, Enfermeras en Hospitales, AGMAV, C. 2802, L. 666, Cp. 5 /4–5.

When Mercedes Milá arrived in Salamanca, such problems were widely discussed by Health Service officials. Some proposed asking the Red Cross to coordinate female auxiliary staff, others called for an independent solution. The inspector general of the Health Service proposed a whole set of rules for the admission and deployment of female staff but also called for a person responsible for the women in the Health Service.[71] A transferal of this kind of responsibility to the Francoist Red Cross was, however, out of the question. The negotiations with the ICRC had been complicated enough due to the Republican government's always being quick to accuse the ICRC of legitimizing Francoists by accepting their Red Cross committee. The "humanitarian peace" between the warring factions was fragile and Francoists had an interest in keeping it that way.[72] In this context, Mercedes Milá reached the General Headquarters and offered her help to Franco, instead of joining the Francoist SRC. In this way, she took a meaningful and political decision which worked out in her favor. A few months later, on 24 March 1937, "by order of His Excellency," Mercedes Milá was named "Inspector General of all female staff – professional, auxiliary, and voluntary – in the hospitals." She was charged with the responsibility to "propose transferals, admissions, and dismissals" but also to "provide the officials of the Health Service with the number of staff necessary to complete their mission."[73] She became the "only woman to officially join the Generalíssimo's General Headquarters; she even wore the corresponding regimental badge on her uniform."[74] Published in the official law gazette, Mercedes Milá not only became the first official Francoist nurse but was also given the responsibility of defining what a Francoist nurse was supposed to be.

Before the Civil War, Mercedes Milá had reached the glass ceiling of female career pathways in nursing in Spain. The Civil War marked a turning point for her. It was the beginning of Franco's dictatorship – a political system born out of the violence of a Civil War waged by the insurgent armed forces. With the army in power and mass warfare on the ground, a Health Service reform was necessary, and with it the role of the military nurse was created. By choosing Franco over the SRC, she left her peers behind and took on an outstanding position in the Francoist healthcare system.

---

71 Cuartel General del Generalísimo, Estado Mayor, Enfermeras en Hospitales, AGMAV, C. 2802, L. 666, Cp. 5 /6–7.
72 García López, *Entre el odio y la venganza*, 21–23.
73 Boletín Oficial del Estado, 26.03.1937, N° 157.
74 Fundación Nacional Francisco Franco, Mercedes Milá Nolla.

IV. A Question of Power: Being the 'Head of All the Nurses'

The first task for Mercedes Milá was not only to set up a nurses' corps but to assert her power over the female staff deployed in the Health Service. Her appointment as inspector general came at a moment when Franco laid, by decree, important cornerstones for building the 'new' Spanish society. Franco legitimized his claim to power with the promise that he would 'restore order'. This narrative served to delegitimize the Second Republic and to blame its government for what Francoists perceived as the reigning social 'chaos' and the threat of becoming a victim of 'Soviet communism and revolution.' It also served to promote 'order' as rule by a strong leader, complementary gender roles, and Catholic values.[75] To ensure this new course, measures were taken to cut across cultural and political pluralism. "Efficient government action [...] requires that the individual and collective action of all Spaniards be subordinated to their shared goal. This truth [...] is incompatible with the struggle of political parties and organizations which [...] spend their best energies in the struggle for dominance,"[76] read the preamble to the infamous unification decree of 20 April 1937. This decree ordered that all political parties be dissolved and integrated under the expanded and redefined roof of Falange, now called Falange Española Tradicionalista y de las Juntas de Ofensiva Nacional Sindicalistas, or FET y de las JONS.[77] Henceforward, Francoist Spain officially knew only one army and only one political party, the Falangist party, and Falange – and its women's organization, the Sección Femenina – gained a key position in the formation of the "fascistisized"[78] state Franco was building. In addition, a gendered discourse on wartime division labor intensified. Men were called up to volunteer for combatant duty, and women were mobilized to save the nation in the rearguard.

The unification decree was published only a month after Mercedes Milá began her work as inspector general, when she was busy setting up the army nurses' corps SFSM. The decree triggered a social earthquake among non-military Spanish relief actors. International organizations were not targeted by this unification decree and its consequences. However, the women's organizations linked to other political parties or groups such as the Carlist Margaritas that had

---

75 Rocío López de Castro, "La imagen de la mujer en el siglo XX", in *100 años en femenino. Una historia de las mujeres en España*, ed. by Oliva María Rubio, Isabel Tejeda, (Madrid: Acción Cultural Española, 2012), 149; Mary Nash, "Las mujeres en el último siglo", in: *100 años en femenino. Una historia de las mujeres en España*, ed. by Oliva María Rubio, Isabel Tejeda, (Madrid: Acción Cultural Española, 2012), 25–51, 45–47.
76 Boletín Oficial del Estado, 20. April 1937, N° 182.
77 Ibid.
78 On the concept of "fascistization," see Ismael Saz Campos, "Fascism, Fascistization and Developmentalism in Franco's Dictatorship", *Social History* 29 (2004) 3: 342–357.

set up relief projects during the preceding months faced being integrated into the Sección Femenina of FET y de las JONS from one day to the next.[79] Henceforward, all the various relief projects that had grown grassroots in Francoist society were officially run under the label and rule of the Sección Femenina. Subsequently, relief projects were systematized and ascribed to specific zones of influence, and all medical relief projects that had hitherto catered to the army were sent to the rearguard. While this was in some way a boon for the Sección Femenina, the appointment of Mercedes Milá as inspector general was not, because henceforward only SFSM was to aid the army. This was a blow to the Sección Femenina, which was eager to extend its influence into all female social spaces, as their understanding of Falangism included the totalization of the women's movement.[80] These decrees issued during spring 1937 meant that their access to the armed forces was officially cut off. The situation was similar for the women (and men) of the Francoist Red Cross. The creation of the SFSM reinforced not only the gendered segregation of social spaces of war but also the formal exclusion of political and humanitarian actors from the vanguard.

Frictions and conflict were not long in coming. Mercedes Milá's vast correspondence contains ample evidence of such conflicts over power. Analysis of these letters shows that when Mercedes Milá took up her new position, she was determined to eliminate any competition for her authority. As her key tool for relegating her competitors she used her right, enshrined by decree, to "admit, transfer, and dismiss" staff. Only women who held diplomas from certain schools or who had taken the SFSM course were allowed in.[81] She also used it to launch a general staff inventory, to set up staff files, to create specific symbols such as emblems worn on the uniform, and to create an identity card to distinguish army nurses and auxiliaries from other nurses. This ID came, furthermore, with some privileges. Her staff could, for instance, enter and leave militarized zones and move through the country to their next deployment postings, even after curfew.[82] Her right "to propose transfers, admissions and dismissals" became the backbone of a new administration, privilege distribution, and symbolism, but also a tool for elevating Francoist nurses above all other nurses at the time. Although she used these tools against all her competitors, she nonetheless dealt with them

---

79 Pérez Espí, *Mercedes Sanz-Bachiller*, 103–106.
80 On the Sección Femenina's aspirations, see inter alia Ángela Cenarro Lagunas, "La Falange es un modo de ser (mujer): discursos e identidades de género en las publicaciones de la Sección Femenina (1938–1945)", *Historia y Política. Ideas, Procesos y Movimientos Sociales*, 37 (2017): 91–120.
81 Cuartel General del Generalísimo.- Estado Mayor, Enfermeras en Hospitales, AGMAV, C. 2802, L 666, Cp. 5/6.
82 Cuartel General del Generalísimo.- Estado Mayor, Enfermeras, AGMAV, C. 2744, L 522.

differently. Paradigmatically, I will discuss her relationship with the Francoist SRC and the Falangist Sección Femenina.

The Sección Femenina reacted to these practices of exclusion with hostility. Conflict with them is a consistent thread throughout Mercedes Milá's correspondence. As a staunch advocate of vocational training of nursing according to the international standards of the time, she must have considered the efforts of the Sección Femenina to organize crash courses dilettante and disrespectful of the medical ethos. Most of the time, these frictions and her disregard for the Sección Femenina appeared as little sideswipes or subtle comments, but sometimes incidents grew into conflicts that were not easily resolved. The Sección Femenina showed creativity and determination in undermining Mercedes Milá's position and influence. But the latter was well aware of her power. As a last resort she would reach out to other levels of the military administration and make use of her other right as defined by decree, namely that "the military authorities and heads of the Health Service provide her with all the support she needed to fulfil her mission."[83] Institutional back-up from army officials usually helped her to relegate the Sección Femenina to their spheres and end conflicts to her own satisfaction. Such tactics of conflict resolution showcase that during the Civil War, Franco prioritized the army and the fight over the civilian and non-militarized home front, and this secured Mercedes Milá's privileged position among organizations providing healthcare.

The establishment of mandatory *Servicio Social* (Social Service) for women by the Sección Femenina reflected paradigmatically one of those more intense conflicts between them and Mercedes Milá. Published in the official law gazette on 11 October 1937, Decree 378 ruled that all women aged seventeenth to thirty-five had to do mandatory war duty in the form of "Servicio Social de la Mujer" for at least six months. In theory, this service was intended to ensure that the Sección Femenina had enough staff to carry out and expand their humanitarian project, Auxilio Social.[84] In practice, it caused masses of women to send their applications to Mercedes Milá and her delegates and ask to do their Social Service in the army. The decree remained vague as to whether this was officially an option, and Auxilio Social did nothing to prevent this from happening. On the contrary, the Sección Femenina seems to have used the creation of *Servicio Social* as an opportunity to regain access to the armed forces.

Initially, Mercedes Milá seems to have been unsure how to deal with the consequences of the establishment of *Servicio Social*. Her correspondence shows that some military hospitals accepted this influx of an inexperienced labor force, but also that the presence of *Servicio Social* women caused serious conflicts with

---

83 Boletín Oficial del Estado, 26. 3. 1937, N° 157, p. 811.
84 Pérez Espí, *Mercedes Sanz-Bachiller*, 131–141.

respect to discipline, efficiency, and capability.⁸⁵ *Servicio Social* women often rather obeyed their regional Sección Femenina leader than the head nurse on duty, did not necessarily stick to their shifts, and prioritized activities organized by the Sección Femenina.⁸⁶ Mercedes Milá's provincial and regional delegates turned to her repeatedly, asking for instructions on how to deal with such situations. "The [people in charge of, K. S.] Servicio Social have not realized that this is not the way things can be done in hospitals and that [...] [our work, K. S.] is more delicate than it seems,"⁸⁷ wrote Mercedes Milá in response to the complaints of one of her delegates.

Servicio Social was used not only by the Sección Femenina as a potential backdoor to the military nurses' corps. The conflict was a two-way street. Since *Servicio Social* was mandatory, all women between seventeen and thirty-five received draft-like letters, as did all military nurses and auxiliaries in this age group. Initially, these women then left their posts to do Social Service. "[It] interrupts the efficiency of the hospitals,"⁸⁸ the head of the military hospitals in Badajoz complained in his letter to Mercedes Milá. Others inquired why there was no possibility to accept military duty as a substitute for *Servicio Social*.⁸⁹ Mercedes Milá eventually passed the issue to other administrative levels, but only later she managed to gain support: "I sent you a message via Pura⁹⁰ a few days after the Servicio Social issue had been resolved, and I hope that one of these days the Minister's provision will come out, which has been agreed upon. Of course, work done at our hospitals counts as Servicio Social,"⁹¹ she reassured one of her provincial delegates after her triumph. In another letter she informed her delegate that "the National Delegate of Auxilio Social will receive instructions from the Minister that they are prohibited from intervening in the deployment of military nurses."⁹² This was a tough conflict which took around half a year before the issue was resolved to Mercedes Milá's satisfaction.⁹³ With the help of the army administration and the ministry, she would prevail against the Sección Feminina.

The relationship between Mercedes Milá and the SRC was different. While conflict came in waves with the Sección Femenina, after the initial quarrel

---

85 Correspondencia de la Inspectora General, AGMAV, C. 42068, 1, 2.
86 Correspondencia de la Inspectora General, AGMAV, C. 42067, 2.
87 Correspondencia de la Inspectora General, AGMAV, C. 42068, 1, 2.
88 Ibid.
89 Ibid.
90 María Purificación Saliquet was one of her secretaries.
91 Correspondencia de la Inspectora General, AGMAV, C. 42067, 2.
92 Correspondencia de la Inspectora General, AGMAV, C. 46761, 1.
93 These conflicts continued even years after the civil war was over and the Division of Volunteers was sent to the Eastern front of the Second World War. See in detail Katharina Seibert, *Who Cares? Negotiating Society and Gender at Spain's Sickbeds during the 1930s and 1940s*, Ph.D. Thesis (University of Vienna: 2022), 369–389.

Mercedes Milá and the women of the SRC found a rather stable way to coexist and cooperate. The beginning was, however, similarly conflict-ridden. The current state of the art on the SRC and a preliminary and cursory analysis of some Red Cross reports and military documentation[94] suggest that the Francoist Red Cross assisted the Francoist army where they could despite the fact that they were officially bound to the principle of impartiality. Gabriel Pretus shows that from the very beginning of the Civil War, wherever local Committees of the Spanish Red Cross were available,[95] they attended the early frontlines.[96] Hence, just like the Sección Femenina, when Mercedes Milá was appointed inspector general, the SRC had already set up a medical infrastructure of their own in the rearguard and behind the lines with their own hierarchies of power.[97] For them too, the rise of Mercedes Milá meant a reconfiguration of their zones of interest and influence.

The reconfiguration of the relationship between Mercedes Milá, and by extension the armed forces and the SRC, was complicated, too, but in a different way. In this process, class and social status came into play rather than ideology as was the case with the Sección Femenina. Among the women of the SRC were many who had taken positions as head nurses or coordinating positions in the army Health Service thanks to the initial high demand for qualified staff. In other words, they had biographies similar to Mercedes Milá's. As members of the affluent middle and upper classes and often long-term members of the SRC they felt entitled to their privileged positions in the healthcare hierarchies. The appointment of Mercedes Milá thus threatened their sense of entitlement and status. One such individual was Rosario Bernaldo de Quirós y Luque. At the beginning of the war, she was appointed "head of the female staff of the Army of the Centre" by the latter's general in chief. She had her headquarters in Cáceres and set up a care work infrastructure similar to the one that Mercedes Milá would establish a few months later. Once Mercedes Milá assumed her position, Rosario Bernaldo de Quirós' was officially demoted, something she did not accept without resistance. "[T]he smooth running of women's affairs […] is my sole responsibility because of my official position as Inspector of the Female Services of the Army of the Centre, a position which on 8 December 1936 was made known to all the military hospitals,"[98] she defended herself in a letter to Mercedes Milá,

---

94 Espagne 1936–1939, Organisation du Service Espagne au CICR, Notes – Instructions, CDMH, C. ESCI-001; Cuartel General del Generalísimo.– Estado Mayor, Enfermeras en Hospitales, AGMAV, C. 2802, L 666; Cuartel General del Generalísimo.– Estado Mayor, Enfermeras, AGMAV, C. 2744, L 522.
95 Cuartel General del Generalísimo.– Estado Mayor, Enfermeras en Hospitales, AGMAV, C. 2802, L 666.
96 Pretus, *La ayuda humanitaria en la guerra civil española*, 44–45.
97 Barona Vilar, Perdiguero-Gil, *Health and the War*, 112.
98 AGMAV, C. 42067, 2.

and openly refused to accept Mercedes Milá as her superior. "[T]he circumstances sometimes require that I cannot wait for your prior approval due to the urgency of a situation,"[99] she explained, and she repeated that she had the endorsement of the general of the Army of the Center.[100] Ultimately, all her networks and all her referring to her longer service did not help. Mercedes Milá asserted her rank and Rosario Bernaldo de Quirós lost her battle. Although their initial fights read as substantial and fierce, as the war continued the two of them became close allies.[101]

The fact that Rosario Bernaldo de Quirós too had been appointed by an army general to organize the female staff made the conflict between her and Mercedes Milá complicated; she was no longer simply an SRC member. But whenever the SRC affiliation was clear, conflict could be resolved more cordially because Mercedes Milá could refer not only to her rights but also to the SRC's duty to provide impartial help. On such occasions, Mercedes Milá put on the metaphorical kid gloves to oust other high-ranking SRC members from their positions. In one instance, she wrote letters of appreciation to several SRC head nurses and "congratulated" them on their "marvelous work." She mentioned that they were "held in high regard by the local authorities and by all the staff" and expressed her hope that their "selflessness and patriotism" would continue, as well as their "interest in the welfare and health of the wounded."[102] To her new head nurse she added, "Not only do I have nothing against them, on the contrary, [...] I hope they will continue to serve the cause as presidents of the committees for the protection of hospitals."[103] Of course, Mercedes Milá knew that these Red Cross women were not only capable healthcare workers but also well-versed fundraisers and well connected with the wealthy upper classes in Francoist Spain and beyond. Keeping SRC women on side made sense for many reasons. The SRC not only trained nurses to Mercedes Milá's taste but also, like the ICRC, systematically and continuously raised funds and donations. Francisco Alía Miranda counted a total of 1,223,597.52 Swiss Francs which the ICRC collected from governments, the League of Nations, and other entities over the course of the war. Again, under the pretense of impartiality, the ICRC gave half of this sum to the Francoist SRC over the course of the conflict.[104]

---

99 Ibid.
100 Ibid.
101 Seibert, *Who Cares?*, 263–265.
102 Correspondencia de la Inspectora General, AGMAV, C. 42067, 2.
103 Ibid.
104 The numbers are from Francisco Francisco Alía Miranda, *La otra cara de la guerra: solidaridad y humanitarismo en la España republicana durante la Guerra Civil (1936–1939)*, (Madrid: Sílex 2021), 129.

Mercedes Milá constantly navigated a fragile dynamic of inclusion and exclusion on the personal and the staff level. On the epistemic level, however, the standards of the Red Cross and Rockefeller Foundation prevailed largely unchallenged. Work was organized along lines these institutions promoted as modern. SFSM nurses worked shifts, responsibilities were distributed in a hierarchical and patriarchal manner, and nurses were conceptualized as aides to the practitioners and doctors. SFSM nurses had to have learned certain bodies of medical knowledge and had to have certain care skills. The code of conduct resembled the norms of behavior SRC *Damas Enfermeras* had learned in their formal training since the 1920s.[105] SFSM nurses were to be not only capable health workers, but also obedient towards their superiors, dedicated to their work, and caring with their patients.[106] This conception of bedside nursing was by no means an invention of the SRC but rather resonated with the then contemporary standards for nursing wherever so-called Western medicine was on the rise.

For Mercedes Milá, it was the Spanish Red Cross where she first came into contact with these standards, and the SRC was an important promoter of them in Spain. Mercedes Milá's insistence on systematic training and the exclusion of actors that underestimated the paradigm of modern medicine and nursing must therefore be understood as the continuation of her previous work, which always promoted the nexus between professionalism and formal training. In asserting her position of power, Mercedes Milá not only helped to monopolize and establish female medical care work in the vanguard zones, but also contributed *en passant* to the institutionalization of the role of "professional nurse" as a femininized and regular profession in Spain.

V. On the Springboard of Humanitarianism – Concluding Remarks

Mercedes Milá's story, taken as a case study, shines a light on several overlapping developments. First, her trajectory to becoming a healthcare professional exemplifies how the SRC helped shape nursing into a professional field that attracted and privileged members of the affluent middle- and upper classes prior to the Spanish Civil War. The ties between the Red Cross movement and the social elites were a common phenomenon all over interwar Europe, and Spain was no exception in that sense. Specific to the Spanish constellation was, however, that

---

105 Concha Germán Bes, *Historia de la institución de la enfermería universitaria análisis con una perspectiva de género*, Ph.D. Thesis, Zaragoza 2007, 163–175.
106 López Vallecillo, "Relevancia de la mujer en el bando nacional de la Guerra Civil Española", 430–431.

the SRC became one of few important facilitators for Spanish healthcare workers and medical professionals to participate in international knowledge exchange networks. Without the SRC, Mercedes Milá would not have gained access to the programs of the Rockefeller Foundation and to the latest state of the art in bedside nursing and public health. In seminars at the prestigious Bedford College, she became one member of Spain's small group of first female experts in healthcare and public health. The SRC was the starting point of such careers and of a modern Spanish healthcare system.

Second, Mercedes Milá's story was also exceptional. There were more women like her who passed through the same institutions of professional training who became healthcare experts. But she was the only one who was allowed into the epicenter of Francoist power during the Civil War. This position gave her the power to contribute building early Francoism. In the way she averted the attempts by the Sección Femenina to extend their power and appropriate the field of war nursing and in the way she relegated SRC members to their positions in the rearguard, she echoed Franco's policy of establishing clear-cut responsibilities during the Civil War. Thus, she became a power broker of early Francoism, which prioritized the army and winning the Civil War.

Third, by continuing SRC teachings on nursing training and organization, she contributed to the firm establishment of nursing knowledge in Spain that had emerged and consolidated in the transnational space of international humanitarianism. Although the Civil War had ultimately led to a separation between the Red Cross and the Francoist army, the influence of international organizations as promoters of so-called Western medicine persisted beyond the Civil War in Spain and shaped postwar nursing training. Humanitarianism was therefore her springboard. It was in this field that her career started and offered her access not only to the expert knowledge she drew on but also to the necessary networks. But Francoism was ultimately the context in which she could acquire a position with decision-making power beyond any other woman in Spain's health care – at least for the duration of the war.

Up to 1939, Mercedes Milá's career reads like a linear story of success. Probably her greatest setback occurred, however, only when the Civil War was officially over and Franco demobilized her nurses and dissolved the corps. In times of "peace," the army was to return to an all-men's institution and misogynist politics of complementary gender roles that relegated women to hearth and home. The Sección Femenina seemed to have triumphed. Their relegation to the rear and the home front offered them the opportunity and legitimation to continue their work as a post-war reconstruction agency. But Mercedes Milá did not give up easily. Instead, she fought hard to keep her nurses' corps alive. She soon received a tailwind – unexpectedly – from the Second World War. The deployment of the so-called Blue Division returned the figure of the war nurse to the stage, and Mercedes Milá's second project, *Damas Auxiliares*, rose from the ashes of the former SFSM. In the wake of the deployment of the Blue Division, *Damas Auxiliares* was institutionalized and prevailed as a permanent body of the Spanish army. Still, military nursing would never again become as powerful a player in bedside nursing in Spain as it was during the Civil War. It became a niche populated by like-minded women.

Julia Schulte-Werning

Milk for the Mellah. Infant Health and the Logistics of Post-Holocaust Humanitarian Aid for Jewish Communities in French Morocco

I. Introduction

On May 31, 1953, representatives of the Moroccan Jewish community, internationally operating Jewish aid organizations, and the health department of the French colonial administration gathered at the dispensary La Maternelle-OSE in Casablanca to celebrate the opening of a newly installed milk station, or *biberonnerie* in French. A vibrant port city and an economic center of the French Protectorate, Casablanca was home to Morocco's largest Jewish community in the mid-20th century; nearly 80,000 of Morocco's 250,000 Jews lived there. While the more affluent members of the community lived in the newly built European quarters of the city, poorer families and those who had recently migrated from the countryside mostly resided in the *mellah*, as the traditional Jewish quarters of Moroccan towns were called.[1] The polyclinic where the milk station was housed catered to the *mellah*'s inhabitants and provided healthcare services to children as well as to expectant and nursing mothers. It was run by OSE-Morocco, the Moroccan branch of the internationally operating Jewish healthcare organization *Oeuvre de Secours aux Enfants* (OSE).[2]

---

1 Andre Levy and Daniel Schroeter, "Casablanca," in *Encyclopedia of Jews in the Islamic World*, edited by Norman A. Stillman (Leiden: Brill, 2010). The French Protectorate of Morocco was established in 1912. Morocco was part of the French empire in North Africa together with Algeria (colonized in 1830) and Tunisia (made a protectorate in 1881). A smaller part of Northern Morocco was ruled by Spain, and the city of Tangier was demarcated as International Zone. In 1956 Morocco gained independence. Susan Gilson Miller, *A History of Modern Morocco* (Cambridge: Cambridge University Press, 2013).
2 This article presents findings and preliminary conclusions from my ongoing research on "Jewish Medical Humanitarianism in North Africa from the 1940s to the 1960s" (working title, dissertation project at the University of Vienna). For their helpful comments on earlier versions of this text, I wish to thank Sarah Knoll, Katharina Seibert, Ethell Gershengorin, the participants of two workshops in which I discussed parts of this case study, especially Jaclyn Granick and Elisabeth Röhrlich, and the two anonymous reviewers.

Co-financed by the Dutch committee of the *United Nations Appeal for Children* (UNAC) and the *American Jewish Joint Distribution Committee* (JDC), the new milk-bottling plant turned milk powder imported from the United States into bottles for distribution. The JDC press release reprinted in American Jewish newspapers lauded the facility as "Morocco's most modern milk-bottling plant," consisting of "a dazzling array of stainless steel tanks." The technical procedure of producing milk was described as an abstract and marvelous process: "The powder and purified water are put in at one end and, forty-five minutes later, emerge as milk – sterilized, homogenized, bottled and capped."[3] The inauguration was deemed a success by all parties involved and presented as an important step in the evolution of the OSE-JDC healthcare program in Casablanca. The milk station featured prominently in the following years' activities reports of OSE-Morocco, was called a "model" institution, and accounted for roughly half of the number of milk bottles distributed annually by the OSE centers in French Morocco.[4] Yet setting up this milk station had been marred by several conflicts around funding and logistics, and the inauguration was also met with relief. The UNAC spokesperson congratulated the JDC that after the "endless complications," the building process had finally come to a "happy solution".[5]

The OSE-JDC engagement and the establishment of the milk station formed part of larger Jewish humanitarian efforts of medical aid and community development in Morocco and other parts of North Africa after the Holocaust. Whereas the OSE-JDC activities in Algeria and Libya mostly encompassed emergency aid for refugees and emigrants on their way to Israel, the medical aid evolved into a long-term healthcare program in Morocco and Tunisia. Tracing the logistics of funding and setting up the milk station, I argue, highlights the frictions among locally and internationally operating Jewish organizations competing for their respective realms of authority and sheds light on the broader

---

3 "Milk-Bottling Plant for Children of Casa Mellah," JDC Archives Collection G45–54 Folder MO.76 Item 795352. Differing in title and length, the same text was published in several American Jewish newspapers. "Morocco Ghetto Gets New, Modern Milk-bottling Facilities," The National Jewish Post, June 19, 1953, 7, NLI Newspaper Collection; "JDC Establishes Milk Bottling Plant," The Jewish Community Bulletin, June 19, 1953, 6, NLI Newspaper Collection. For the draft, see Letter from Cohen, undated, JDC Archives Collection G45–54 Folder ORG.193 Item 2136217.

4 F. Mosberg: Information on Health Problems and Programs in French Morocco, American Joint Distribution Committee Medical Conference June 28–July 1, 1954, 9–10, JDC Archives Collection G45–54 Folder MO.90 Item 796592; World Union O.S.E., Reports submitted to the General Assembly July 4th–9th 1957, Part 3 Reports of National Branches, OSE-Morocco, 6, CAHJP Collection Union Mondiale OSE Folder OSE-PAR-10; 1953 Annual Report, The New Geography, The American Jewish Joint Distribution Committee, 7, JDC Archives Collection NY AR194554 Folder 2212 Item 962258.

5 Letter from Walle-Bosch to Gonik, May 30, 1953, JDC Archives Collection G45–54 Folder MO.76 Item 795355.

visions that were tied to providing milk for the infants of the *mellah*. I explore how milk functioned both as a commodity and as a symbol in the post-Holocaust quest to raise a "healthy new generation" in late colonial Morocco and played a central role in positioning Jewish organizations within the landscape of international infant health endeavors. The episode of the milk station in the Jewish community of Casablanca showcases the blurred boundaries between humanitarian and developmental community aid and adds to a more nuanced understanding of postwar international health politics. Based on an analysis of records from the Jewish organizations involved, the article focuses on the actions of the management level of OSE and JDC and provides insight into the inner workings of aid institutions.

The milk station project proves to be as much a story about the negotiation of Jewish futures after the Holocaust in the context of decolonization as about the complex inter-organizational relationships that mark the history of humanitarianism. Historians of humanitarianism and philanthropy have stressed that competition between aid organizations for funding and publicity was one of the dilemmas inherent to modern relief and development activities.[6] Linking forms of aid, reconstruction, and advocacy, modern forms of Jewish humanitarianism oscillated between emergency relief campaigns, diaspora welfare structures, and non-state development projects, as shown by Jaclyn Granick.[7] Adding to the existent scholarship on wartime and postwar Jewish aid for survivors of the Holocaust and for emigrants to Israel, an examination of Jewish medical humanitarianism on behalf of Moroccan Jewry sheds light on the intersections between postwar Europe, Israel, and (post)colonial North Africa.[8] The aid activities of the JDC and OSE provide an entry point into probing the dynamics between local Jewish community structures, transnational diaspora aid net-

---

6 Johannes Paulmann, "The Dilemmas of Humanitarian Aid: Historical Perspectives," in *Dilemmas of Humanitarian Aid in the Twentieth Century*, edited by Johannes Paulmann (Oxford: Oxford University Press, 2016), 28–30. For sociological debates on the reciprocity of aid and philanthropy, see for example Emily Barman, "The Social Bases of Philanthropy," *Annual Review of Sociology* 43 (2017): 271–290.
7 Jaclyn Granick, *International Jewish Humanitarianism in the Age of the Great War* (Cambridge: Cambridge University Press, 2021), 14–22 and 299–300; Abigail Green, "Religious Internationalisms," in *Internationalisms: A Twentieth-Century History*, edited by Glenda Sluga and Patricia Clavin (Cambridge: Cambridge University Press, 2017), 24–27; Jonathan Dekel-Chen, "Activism as Engine: Jewish Internationalism, 1880s–1980s," in *Religious Internationals in the Modern World: Globalization and Faith Communities since 1750*, edited by Abigail Green and Vincent Viaene (Basingstoke Palgrave Macmillan, 2021), 269–276.
8 On postwar Jewish reconstruction in Europe, see for example Laura Hobson Faure, *A Jewish Marshall Plan: The American Jewish Presence in Post-Holocaust France* (Bloomington: Indiana University Press, 2022). On the intersections between Jewish history and the history of empire, see Ethan Katz et al. (eds.), *Colonialism and the Jews* (Bloomington: Indiana University Press, 2017).

works, and international bodies in postwar French Morocco on the verge of decolonization.

The quest for a modern milk station supplying Moroccan Jewish children in need can also be seen as epitomizing the postwar milk boom, which peaked in the early 1950s and in which larger trends in the field of maternal and infant healthcare and in the internationalization of health converged. In the aftermath of World War II, milk – and especially milk powder – assumed an unprecedented role in international emergency feeding programs and development schemes. It turned into a staple, first of emergency feeding programs for war-torn Europe and Asia conducted by organizations like UNRRA or CARE, and then of late colonial development projects in cooperation with new international bodies like UNICEF and international corporations.[9] Looking at milk therefore provides an entry point into the discussion of global health at the intersection of postwar reconstruction, colonial welfare politics, and decolonization.[10] While recent research on postwar feeding programs has emphasized the role of international organizations, colonial administrations, and Christian philanthropies, an analysis of Jewish organizations further contributes to our understanding of transnational and international networks of humanitarianism and development.

II. Why Milk Mattered

After World War II, the living conditions of Moroccan Jews became a major concern to both local and international Jewish organizations, especially regarding the state of children growing up in poverty in the *mellah*. First introduced to Fez in the 15th century and gradually created in other towns, the *mellah* had eventually become a symbol of the impoverished state of the Moroccan Jewish

---

9 Samuël Coghe, "Between Colonial Medicine and Global Health: Protein Malnutrition and UNICEF Milk in the Belgian Congo," *Medical History* 65 (2021): 384–402; Shobana Shankar, "Blurring Relief and Development: Religious and Secular Politics of International Humanitarian Intervention during Decolonization in Sub-Saharan Africa," in *Dilemmas of Humanitarian Aid in the Twentieth Century*, edited by Johannes Paulmann (Oxford: Oxford University Press, 2016), 263–288; Heike Wieters, "Reinventing the Firm: From Post-War Relief to International Humanitarian Agency," *European Review of History: Revue européenne d'histoire* 23 (2016): 116–135; Frederick Cooper, "Writing the History of Development," *Journal of Modern European History* 8 (2010): 5–23.

10 Jennifer Johnson, *The Battle for Algeria: Sovereignty, Health Care, and Humanitarianism* (Philadelphia: University of Pennsylvania Press, 2016); Jessica Lynne Pearson, *The Colonial Politics of Global Health: France and the United Nations in Postwar Africa* (Cambridge: Harvard University Press, 2018); Ellen J. Amster, *Medicine and the Saints: Science, Islam, and the Colonial Encounter in Morocco, 1877–1956* (Austin: University of Texas Press, 2014).

population to European visitors in the 19th century.[11] This notion was propelled by French colonial rule and rapid urbanization in the early 20th century, which fostered overcrowded and hazardous living conditions amongst poorer populations, both Muslim and Jewish.[12] In the French Protectorate, welfare and healthcare were fragmented along the lines of the colonial population categories "European", "Muslim", and "Jewish". As part of France's "civilizing mission", medicine and hygiene were avenues of disciplining and "modernizing" the local population. Although the health of Europeans was a priority, the Protectorate administration expanded healthcare for Moroccans after World War II to counter anti-colonial mobilization against their rule. In parallel, Muslim and Jewish organizations provided welfare for the poor. Yet the capacities for non-European and impoverished population groups remained precarious.[13] When JDC delegates visited the Casablanca *mellah* in late 1948, they emphasized the gap between reading about the living conditions and witnessing them first-hand:

> "It is one thing to read that TB and trachoma are widespread, it is another to see child after child going blind, dying of disease and hunger, living in filth and ignorance. Nearly 50% of deaths among native Moroccan Jews in Casablanca are of children under 2; this is a statistic whose unfolding is difficult to witness."[14]

Overcrowded housing, lack of air and light, prevalence of infectious diseases, high infant mortality and inadequate childcare were the cornerstones of the

---

11 Emily Benichou Gottreich, "On the Origins of the Mellah of Marrakesh," *International Journal of Middle East Studies* 35 (2003): 287–288; Daniel J. Schroeter, "How Jews became 'Moroccan'," in *From Catalonia to the Caribbean: The Sephardic Orbit from Medieval to Modern Times*, edited by Federica Francesconi et al. (Leiden: Brill, 2018), 224; Emily Benichou Gottreich, *Jewish Morocco: A History from Pre-Islamic to Postcolonial Times* (London: Bloomsbury, 2021), 104–108 and 116–123.
12 Miller, *A History of Modern Morocco*, 93–119.
13 Amster, *Medicine and the Saints*, 129–131 and 183–208; Miller, *A History of Modern Morocco*, 139–140 and 146–147; Jonathan G. Katz, "Jewish Bodies, Muslim Bodies, and French Medicine in Morocco," in *Jews and Muslims in Morocco: Their Intersecting Worlds*, edited by Joseph Chetrit et al. (Lanham: Lexington Books, 2021), 128–130; Daniel River, "Hygiènisme colonial et médicalisation de la société marocaine au temps du protectorat français (1912–1956)," in *Santé, medicine et société dans le monde arabe*, edited by Elisabeth Longuenesse (Lyon: Maison de l'Orient et de la Méditerranée, 1995), 105–128; Antoine Perrier, "Les sociétés de bienfaisance musulmane au Maroc: Fiscalité, dons et subventions publiques dans le financement de l'action contre la pauvreté (années 1920–années 1950)," *Revue d'histoire de la protection sociale* 15 (2022): 48–71. On British and French late colonial development, see Frederick Cooper, "Development, Modernization, and the Remaking of an Imperial World Order," in *Perspectives on the History of Global Development*, edited by Corinna R. Unger et al. (Berlin: De Gruyter, 2022), 93–84.
14 Letter from Stein to Schwartz and Beckelman, October 9, 1948, Appendix "Report on Visit to French Morocco, September 18th-28th, 1948," 2, JDC Archives Collection G45-54 Folder NA.37 Item 798571.

accounts circulating between Moroccan and international Jewish organizations in the mid- to late 1940s.

Intertwined with these concerns was the ambiguous legal status of Moroccan Jews in the Protectorate as part of the colonial category of the so-called "indigenous" population.[15] As the Moroccan national movement gained momentum after World War II, the question of how integrative the "Moroccan nation" would be towards Moroccan Jews was contentious, especially in the context of rising anti-Zionism and antisemitism. With the tensions in Palestine and the subsequent Arab–Israeli War in 1948, anti-Jewish riots in Morocco and other parts of North Africa jeopardized the safety of Jews in the region. Against the backdrop of political insecurities, the upsurge of anti-Jewish violence, and socioeconomic turmoil, the majority of Morocco's Jewish population eventually left for Israel and elsewhere over the course of the next two decades. This emigration movement was part of the unfolding exodus of Jews from the Middle East and North Africa.[16] In the late 1940s and the 1950s, the fate of North African Jews thus was an increasingly pressing question for Jewish organizations across the world,[17] and OSE-Morocco's medical aid program was part of this dynamic.

In the interwar period, OSE had transformed from a Russian Jewish social medicine organization to a European and worldwide network of childcare organizations. The OSE network consisted of national branches, linked through the umbrella organization OSE-Union.[18] After the landing of the Allied troops had ended Vichy rule in French Morocco in November 1942 and Vichy policies were gradually revoked, Moroccan Jewish leaders pressed for the engagement of international Jewish organizations on behalf of Moroccan Jewry.[19] OSE was

---

15 Schroeter, "How Jews became 'Moroccan'," 235–239.
16 Miller, *A History of Modern Morocco*, 159–160; Gottreich, *Jewish Morocco*, 148–168; Michael M. Laskier, "Developments in the Jewish Communities of Morocco 1956–76," *Middle Eastern Studies* 26 (1990): 465–505; Dario Miccoli, "The Jews of the Middle East and North Africa: A Historiographic Debate," *Middle Eastern Studies* 56 (2020): 511–520. On Moroccan Jewish political affiliations, see Rachel Heckman, *The Sultan's Communists: Moroccan Jews and the Politics of Belonging* (Stanford: Stanford University Press, 2020).
17 Nathan Kurz, *Jewish Internationalism and Human Rights after the Holocaust* (Cambridge: Cambridge University Press, 2021), 86–111; Maud S. Mandel, *Muslims and Jews in France: History of a Conflict* (Princeton: Princeton University Press, 2014), 35–42.
18 OSE-Union had been founded in Berlin in 1923 and was displaced to Paris in the advent of National Socialism and then further to Geneva during the war. In the postwar years OSE-Union returned to Paris. Laura Hobson Faure et al. (eds.): *L'Oeuvre de Secours aux Enfants et les populations juives au XXe siècle: Prévenir et guérir dans un siècle de violences* (Paris: Colin, 2014); Nadav Davidovitch and Rakefet Zalashik, "'Air, Sun, Water': Ideology and Activities of OZE (Society for the Preservation of the Health of the Jewish Population) During the Interwar Period," *Dynamis* 28 (2008): 127–149; Granick, *International Jewish Humanitarianism*, 165–166 and 186–193.
19 Susan Gilson Miller, *Years of Glory: Nelly Benatar and the Pursuit of Justice in Wartime North Africa* (Stanford 2021), 9–23 and 135–137; Ariel Danan, "Régénérer les Juifs du Maroc et de

amongst the bodies they addressed. In the immediate postwar years, the war-torn remainders of OSE focused on the suffering of Jewish survivors in Europe, but eventually redirected an increasing share of its resources to North Africa and the young State of Israel. A first Moroccan OSE committee was founded in Casablanca in 1945 and the healthcare activities started in 1947.[20]

In the late 1940s, OSE-Morocco became the body through which the JDC channeled most of its medical aid for Moroccan Jews. Decidedly shaping international Jewish humanitarianism, the JDC had been founded as an emergency relief organization in 1914 and fused American progressivist ideals of efficient management and modern social welfare approaches with a profound sense of Jewish solidarity. The JDC's policy was to work with and through local bodies and to eventually render the communities as self-sufficient as possible.[21] The JDC and OSE had worked together since the aftermath of World War I. In Morocco, the JDC had first been active in relief for Jewish refugees from Europe during World War II. With the upsurge of anti-Jewish violence in the late 1940s, the JDC committed itself to an extensive aid program for the local Jewish population and a long-term activity in the region, which encompassed healthcare, education, and material aid.[22] OSE-Morocco was then also equipped with a management level of JDC-recruited public health experts.[23]

Casablanca – where the continuous influx of internal and transit migrants kept the Jewish population relatively stable throughout the 1950s – was the center of OSE-Morocco's activities, both in terms of the leadership structure and the scope of medical services and facilities.[24] The evolving medical program of OSE-Morocco was shaped by the long trajectory of social medicine that the OSE

Tunisie: La coopération entre l'OSE et l'AIU après 1945," in *L'Oeuvre de Secours aux Enfants et les populations juives au XXe siècle: Prévenir et guérir dans un siècle de violences*, edited by Laura Hobson Faure et al. (Paris: Colin, 2014), 268. On the francophone socialization of Moroccan Jewish reformers, see Jessica Marglin, "Modernizing Moroccan Jews: The AIU Alumni Association in Tangier, 1893–1913," *The Jewish Quarterly Review* 101 (2011): 574–603; Mohammed Kenbib, "Levy, Samuel-Daniel," in *Encyclopedia of Jews in the Islamic World*, edited by Norman A. Stillman (Leiden: Brill, 2010); Gottreich, *Jewish Morocco*, 115–126.

20 Letter from Lévy to OSE Union, March 11, 1946, YIVO Archives RG 494 Folder 458; L'Oeuvre de l'O.S.E. au Maroc, in: OSE-Maroc Année 1950, 4–7, CAHJP Collection Union Mondiale OSE Folder OSE-PAR-316.
21 Granick, *International Jewish Humanitarianism*, 8–24; Hobson Faure, *A Jewish Marshall Plan*, 77–100.
22 Miller, *Years of Glory*, 31–128 and 153–158. On the OSE–JDC negotiations on how to structure their collaboration in North Africa in 1948 and 1949, see for example, Deuxième mission en Afrique du Nord, Janvier-Fevrier 1949, Rapport du Dr. H. Fajerman, YIVO Archives RG 494 Folder 1199.
23 Points Concerning the Appointment of Dr. Ernest Raphael to Union-OSE, December 22, 1949, JDC Archives Collection G45-54 Folder MO.193 Item 2136313.
24 General Report on the Activities of O.S.E. July 1950-July 1952, 61 and 63, JDC Archives Collection G45-54 Folder ORG.191 Item 2136182.

network had fostered since its inception and the JDC's expertise in US public health and social work models. OSE-Morocco offered general medical consultations for children and preventive healthcare for expectant mothers and newborns. Health workers conducted mass screenings and treatments of tinea, trachoma, and tuberculosis, and built up a school hygiene program.[25] These medical services also served to facilitate emigration to Israel.[26]

Overall, the various advocacy groups and aid bodies for the Jewish community faced a predicament, as was frequently discussed in the late 1940s and early 1950s: most agreed on the fact that the living conditions in the *mellah* were the root cause for many of the medical and social issues, yet building new housing exceeded the capacities of these private organizations. As long as the Protectorate administration and the Jewish community committees did not find a remedy for the housing issue, medical and other aid programs were to be limited in their long-term efficacy. Since this issue could not be resolved soon, however, medical aid was also even more urgent and important.[27]

The new milk station in the Casablanca dispensary La Maternelle-OSE was not in itself the beginning of milk distribution. It had been a part of the medical program of OSE-Morocco since the beginning of its activities in 1947. Its sister branch, OSE-Tunisia, also ran milk distribution services as part of its maternal and infant health program.[28] Handed out as ready-made bottles, so-called *biberons* in French, or as milk powder to be prepared at home, milk was used as a tool to combat and prevent malnutrition and digestive illnesses among newborns and infants, as a supplement to support the diet of pregnant or nursing women,

---

25 See for example, "Le travail social des œuvres juives de Casablanca", CAHJP Collection Union Mondiale OSE Folder OSE-PAR-68. On the JDC-OSE campaign against trachoma, see Anat Mooreville, "Oculists in the Orient: A History of Trachoma, Zionism, and Global Health, 1882–1973," unpublished PhD thesis, University of California, 2015, 134–178.

26 Benny Nuriely, "[Hebr.] We Must Save the Children: The Organization OSE and North African Jews," in [Hebr.] *Zionism and Empire: הציונות והאימפריה*, edited by Yehuda Shenhav (Jerusalem: The Van Leer Jerusalem Institute, 2015), 269–300; Avi Picard, "Immigration, Health and Social Control: Medical Aspects of the Policy Governing Aliyah from Morocco and Tunisia, 1951–54," *The Journal of Israeli History* 22 (2003): 32–60.

27 S.D. Lévy: Notes sur la situation des juifs du Mellah, January 1, 1946, 1, YIVO Archives RG 494 Folder 457; "En faveur de l'Habitat Israëlite," NOAR Nr. 15–16, March-April 1948, NLI Newspaper Collection; Letter from Stein to Schwartz and Beckelman, October 9, 1948, Appendix "Report on Visit to French Morocco, September 18th–28th, 1948," 6, JDC Archives Collection G45-54 Folder NA.37 Item 798571; "Les leaders du judaisme marocain decident une Action Commune. Important exposé de M. Bein directeur de l'AJDC sur le travail social au Maroc," NOAR Nr. 26, February 16, 1950, NLI Newspaper Collection.

28 Rapport General sur les Activitiés de l'O.S.E. Juillet 1952–Juillet 1954, Présenté à la Conference Mondiale O.S.E. 1954, 93, CAHJP Collection Union Mondiale OSE Folder OSE-PAR-1. In the interwar period, the JDC and the OSE branches had run milk distribution services in Jewish communities in Eastern Europe. See Davidovitch and Zalashik, "'Air, Sun, Water'," 127–149; Granick, *International Jewish Humanitarianism*, 150–196.

and as a cornerstone of feeding programs for school children. As highlighted at its inauguration, the milk station in Casablanca was used for producing a variety of "medicinal milks [des laits médicamenteux]" that could be enriched with various properties according to the doctor's prescription.[29] Milk thus assumed a dual role between food and medicine.

With its new milk station, OSE-Morocco inscribed itself in a set of practices of maternal and infant welfare that had evolved in the late 19th century. Centers for the distribution of milk, so-called *gouttes de lait* or milk drops, had emerged in France in the late 19th century and soon became part of the canon of maternal and infant healthcare services for working-class women across Europe and America. What constituted adequate infant feeding, however, was a contested field, and the value of breastfeeding vis-à-vis other practices of infant feeding like the gradually commodified bottle-feeding was continuously debated among experts in the early 20th century.[30] In colonial contexts, maternal and infant healthcare services and *gouttes de lait* became focal points of state policy and private initiatives that emerged in the interwar period to tackle the high rates of infant mortality seen as a demographic threat.[31] In the aftermath of World War II, milk and milk powder were central commodities in international aid. In the emergency feeding programs for war-torn Europe and Asia, nutrition sciences and the surplus of milk powder from the United States shaped the focus on milk as key source of protein,

---

29 Inauguration Biberonnerie. Discours Dr. Benzaquen, 1, JDC Archives Collection G45–54 Folder MO.76 Item 795346. The milk station produced whole milk, half-cream milk, and lactic acid milk. The production capacity steadily increased, reaching a monthly total of 27,475 bottles of whole milk by the end of 1953. Letter from Mosberg to AJDC Health Department, November 5, 1953, JDC Archives Collection G45–54 Folder MO.76 Item 795320; Letter from Mosberg to AJDC Health Department, January 11, 1954, JDC Archives G45–54 Folder MO.76 Item 795315; Letter from Hurwitz to AJDC Paris, July 30, 1953, Appendix "Report of the Organization of the Milk Station," 1, JDC Archives Collection G45–54 Folder MO.76 Item 795327.

30 Catherine Rollet, "La santé et la protection de l'enfant vues à travers les congrès internationaux (1880–1920)," *Annales de démographie historique* 101 (2001): 102–110; Cécile Lestienne, "Lutter contre la tuberculose et la mortalité infantile: L'établissement des dispensaires en France (1880–1950)," *In Situ* 31 (2017): 2–3; Larry Frohman, "Prevention, Welfare, and Citizenship: The War on Tuberculosis and Infant Mortality in Germany, 1900–1930," *Central European History* 39 (2006): 449–466 and 477–478; Gal Ventura, "'Long Live the Bottle': The Rise of the French Bottle-feeding Industry in the Nineteenth Century," *Social History of Medicine* 32 (2019): 329–356; Rima D. Apple, *Mothers and Medicine: A Social History of Infant Feeding* (Madison: University of Wisconsin Press, 1987), 35–49 and 150–166.

31 Samuël Coghe, *Population Politics in the Tropics: Demography, Health and Transimperialism in Colonial Angola* (Cambridge: Cambridge University Press, 2022), 178–205; Nancy Rose Hunt, "'Le Bebe en Brousse': European Women, African Birth Spacing and Colonial Intervention in Breast Feeding in the Belgian Congo," *The International Journal of African Historical Studies* 21 (1988), 402–410 and 419–423.

as James A. Gillespie highlights.³² Once the immediate aftermath of the war was over, international organizations shifted their aid projects towards colonies and recently independent countries in sub-Saharan Africa and other regions.³³ The "model" milk station in Casablanca formed part of these dynamics. The protracted process of installing it sheds light on how the logistics of postwar Jewish and non-Jewish aid networks worked between Europe, America, and North Africa.

III. Bringing the Machinery to Morocco

Planning the milk station brought together humanitarian actors from North Africa, Europe, and America who all agreed on the value of such an institution. Funding the equipment for the milk station and installing it, however, proved to be a process infused with struggles over organizational collaboration and leadership. Tied to the evolution of the overall OSE–JDC healthcare program in Morocco, the process of bringing the machinery to Morocco showcases the complex logistics of Jewish medical humanitarianism in postwar North Africa and the strained cooperation between various aid organizations.

Throughout the 1950s, the collaboration between OSE-Morocco, OSE-Union, and the JDC was marked by tensions over how to define and demarcate their realms of activities and authorities. The postwar OSE network consisted of branches that focused on relief work, such as in France, Israel, Morocco and Tunisia, and branches mostly occupied with fundraising, based in Western Europe, North and South America, and South Africa.³⁴ By far surpassing OSE funds, local donations, and subventions from the authorities, most of OSE-Morocco's budget was covered by the JDC.³⁵ OSE-Union itself, too, relied upon subventions from the JDC. This gave the JDC considerable leverage in shaping the aid programs. Against this backdrop, the question as to which organization accounted

---

32 James A. Gillespie, "International Organizations and the Problem of Child Health, 1945–1960," *Dynamis* 23 (2003): 122–140; Silvia Inaudi, "'Milk is Life': Nutritional Interventions and Child Welfare: The Italian Case and Post-War International Aid," in *Proteins, Pathologies and Politics: Dietary Innovation and Disease from the Nineteenth Century*, edited by David Gentilcore and Matthew Smith (London: Bloomsbury Academic, 2019), 149–160.
33 Coghe, "Between Colonial Medicine and Global Health," 384–402; Hunt, "'Le Bebe en Brousse'," 424–430; Shankar, "Blurring Relief and Development," 268–279; Lola Wilhelm, "'One of the Most Urgent Problems to Solve': Malnutrition, Trans-Imperial Nutrition Science, and Nestlé's Medical Pursuits in Late Colonial Africa," *The Journal of Imperial and Commonwealth History* 48 (2020): 914–933.
34 Compte Rendu de la Conférence Mondiale O.S.E. 1952, Session Plénière de la Direction Centrale, JDC Archives Collection G45–54 Folder ORG.186 Item 2135574.
35 Recettes et dépenses de l'O.S.E.-Maroc pour l'Année 1950, in: OSE-Maroc Année 1950, 12, CAHJP Collection Union Mondiale OSE Folder OSE-PAR-316.

for or took credit for which accomplishments was a constant bone of contention between OSE-Union and the JDC. Sentiments that one partner downplayed the other's contribution to the aid program were professed by both headquarters. Frequently, OSE-Union would criticize that "in some of its publicity, AJDC [JDC, J.S.] takes all the credit for work accomplished, without sometimes even mentioning the name of OSE."[36] These dynamics also characterized the process of building the new milk-bottling plant for the Casablanca dispensary and decidedly marked the process of bringing the machinery to Morocco.

OSE-Union was initially able to pursue the establishment of a milk station in Casablanca due to fundraising efforts in the Netherlands, which served as confirmation to the OSE network that it was indeed a successful fundraising and coordinating body. In 1950, the Dutch OSE committee succeeded in attracting the interest of the Dutch committee of UNAC and received a donation of 100,000 Dutch guilders. Two thirds were dedicated to OSE-Israel. The remaining 35,000 guilders were devoted to a milk station in Morocco. The donation came with the condition that the equipment was to be Dutch-manufactured, pointing to the commodity character of the machinery and the economic interest tying together international aid projects and donations. Consequently, all the equipment and machinery were ordered from the Oostwoud company, a Dutch producer of medical furniture and equipment located in the northern town of Franeker.[37] At meetings of the OSE network, winning the UNAC's support was recounted as one of the successes of the Dutch OSE, attesting to the raison d'être of those OSE branches focused on fundraising.[38]

However, further developments did not run smoothly and soon tested the ability of OSE-Union to act as a coordinating body. The JDC and OSE-Morocco management became increasingly impatient with the way the OSE-Union headquarters in Paris and the Dutch OSE committee handled the planning for the milk station. By late 1950, OSE-Morocco Medical Director Ernest Raphael inquired about the overall schedule and pointed to the still unresolved questions

---

36 General Report on the Activities of O.S.E. July 1952–July 1954, 42, JDC Archives Collection G45–54 Folder ORG.527 Item 2545303.
37 Coupures de presse sur l'OSE, CAHJP Collection Union Mondiale OSE Folder OSE-PAR-291; Letter from Raphael to Union-OSE, August 22, 1952, JDC Archives Collection G45–54 Folder MO.76 Item 795407; General Report on the Activities of O.S.E. July 1950-July 1952, 64 and 110, JDC Archives Collection G45–54 Folder ORG.191 Item 2136182. The UNAC had been founded in 1948 as a first worldwide campaign to raise funds for newly founded UNICEF. Randall M. Packard, *A History of Global Health: Interventions into the Lives of Other Peoples* (Baltimore: Johns Hopkins University Press, 2016), 126–127.
38 Rapport sur l'activité de l'Union-O.S.E. du 1. 10. 1950 au 1. 12. 1950. Présenté à la Réunion du Comité Exécutif de l'Union-O.S E. du 10 Décembre 1950 par le Dr. M. Prywes, 16, CAHJP Collection Union Mondiale OSE Folder OSE-PAR-3; General Report on the Activities of O.S.E. July 1950–July 1952, 110, JDC Archives Collection G45–54 Folder ORG.191 Item 2136182.

regarding the placement of the milk station and the long-term maintenance budget.[39] The JDC Casablanca office similarly complained that this "lack of action" on the part of OSE proved "rather detrimental to our public relations here."[40]

The communication and coordination between the various offices involved became more and more fraught. In July 1951, the OSE-Union headquarters announced the arrival in Morocco of the Dutch engineer J. Oostwoud, who would be in charge of installing the *biberonnerie*.[41] Yet by the end of the year, planning for the milk station had still not advanced, and Oostwoud left Raphael's several pressing inquiries about the state of affairs unanswered.[42] According to the head of the JDC Health Department in Paris, Alexander Gonik, in a phone call, Oostwoud had declared that "everything is OK," without telling him "a single thing about what 'everything' might be."[43] Raphael's increasingly indignant appeals to OSE-Union for more information on the situation and on when to expect the delivery of the milk station equipment was met with replies he deemed insufficient.[44] By early 1952, JDC Country Director for Morocco, William Bein, was "quite ready to sue him [Oostwoud, J.S.]" and to hand over the matter to the Dutch consul, as he was eagerly waiting for a full account of the facts.[45]

Finally, the JDC offices pieced together the information on the "Oostwoud affair," as it was now referred to in the correspondence. Not only had Oostwoud privately borrowed a considerable sum from OSE-Morocco during his visit in August 1951 and not paid it back, but the overall funding was also at risk. Gonik explained to Bein that when the UNAC donation, "collected on the streets of Amsterdam," had been handed over to OSE-Union, the latter, "in their usual fashion, mishandled the matter" by placing an order for a *biberonnerie* with Oostwoud and paying in advance. With legal procedures hardly promising any success in retrieving the funds, Gonik concluded his letter with a cynical proverb:

---

39 Letter from Raphael to Union-OSE, September 22, 1950, JDC Archives Collection G45–54 Folder MO.76 Item 795447. See also Memorandum from Raphael to Union OSE, Activities 1950/51, April 5, 1951, 37, JDC Archives Collection G45–54 Folder MO.32 Item 792602.
40 Letter from Bein to Janis, December 7, 1950, JDC Archives Collection G45–54 Folder MO.76 Item 795446.
41 Letter from Fajerman to OSE-Maroc, July 18, 1951, JDC Archives Collection G45–54 Folder MO.76 Item 795429.
42 Letter from Raphael to Oostwoud, December 10, 1951, JDC Archives Collection G45–54 Folder MO.76 Item 795438.
43 Letter from Gonik to Raphael, December 12, 1951, attached to Letter from Raphael to Union-OSE, December 31, 1951, JDC Archives Collection G45–54 Folder MO.76 Item 795436.
44 Letter from Raphael to Fajerman, January 8, 1952, JDC Archives Collection G45–54 Folder MO.76 Item 795435.
45 Letter from Bein to Gonik, February 19, 1952, JDC Archives Collection G45–54 Folder MO.76 Item 795431.

"I believe you will agree with me there is little to be done except perhaps 'to believe in God and trust no man'."[46]

To the JDC offices, this matter confirmed the belief in their own capacity of efficient management and planning. In response to Gonik, Bein expressed his exasperation at how the communication had been handled by OSE-Union over the past weeks and months and how they were now left with no funds and no milk station despite the pressing need for one:

> "I wish we could expose Mr Oostwoud and the people who gave him the money in advance to three days' dehydration caused by diarrhoea which could be prevented with a few bottles of milk, if there would be a Biberonnerie. Frankly speaking, I only wish we could say that there is no UNAC – no OSE-Union – and no Mr. Oostwoud, and they would let us make the Biberonnerie for the sake of the children here."[47]

His wish to streamline the whole process by leaving behind the complicated collaboration with the UNAC and OSE-Union and to turn the matter into a JDC-led project reflected a wider sentiment shared by many JDC officials. As Laura Hobson Faure shows in her study on the JDC's work in rebuilding the Jewish communities in post-Holocaust France, the relationship between the JDC and the local French Jewish organizations – including OSE-France – were marked by different understandings of efficient management and, importantly, a reversal of the prewar roles of the French organizations. French Jewish organizations were no longer providers of aid, but themselves dependent on outside assistance.[48] In this context, the milk station "affair" was part of a re-negotiation of the international landscape of postwar Jewish humanitarianism It reaffirmed the position of American Jewish organizations, and especially the JDC, as major funding and coordinating bodies of international Jewish aid vis-à-vis the European Jewish networks which had been shattered by the Holocaust.

Eventually, the project was indeed led by the JDC. Over the next months, Gonik reached an agreement with the UNAC according to which the latter's original grant of 35,000 Dutch guilders would be made available to the JDC, and the JDC would cover any exceeding expenses as well as the long-term maintenance costs of the milk station. The contract with Oostwoud was cancelled, and the JDC

---

46 Letter from Gonik to Bein, February 22, 1952, JDC Archives Collection G45–54 Folder MO.76 Item 795430; see also Letter from Gonik to Accounting Department, February 4, 1952, JDC Archives Collection G45–54 Folder MO.76 Item 795432. For the original order placed by the Dutch OSE committee, see Centrale biberonnière déstinée à Casablanca, January 8, 1951, JDC Archives Collection G45–54 Folder MO.77 Item 795521.
47 Letter from Bein to Gonik, February 27, 1952, 2, JDC Archives Collection G45–54 Folder MO.76 Item 795428.
48 Hobson Faure, A Jewish Marshall Plan, 16–39, 89–92 and 143–144.

would take over the project development and implementation.⁴⁹ Meanwhile, the JDC's negotiations with OSE-Union and Oostwoud regarding the pending expenses continued; in September the Dutch JDC office informed Gonik that the borrowed money had been "obtained", concluding this part of the affair.⁵⁰ By then, two years had passed since the initial idea and the UNAC grant for a new milk station in the Casablanca dispensary, and all parties involved were eager to bring the project to a conclusion.

In fall 1952, the concrete planning for the milk station gained momentum, and the various stakeholders finally worked together more smoothly. The technical details of the milk production plant were developed between the OSE-Morocco medical director and the JDC office in Casablanca, the JDC Health Department in Paris, the JDC Supply Division in New York, and a technical bureau in the Netherlands newly hired for planning and assembling the plant. Between fall 1952 and spring 1953, the various departments were in close contact to clarify the technical details, to determine the exact composition of the machinery and the criteria for installing it, and to conduct the necessary construction work.⁵¹ While the machinery came from the Netherlands, the JDC Supply Division also reached out to other European and American manufacturers to find suitable nipple caps for the bottles, for instance.⁵² The milk powder itself was mostly derived from donations that the JDC received from the US Department of Agriculture.⁵³ Once the milk station was up and running, the JDC was also in contact with Dutch,

---

49 Letter from Acohen to Gonik, August 14, 1952, JDC Archives Collection G45–54 Folder MO.76 Item 795410; Letter from Gonik to Walle-Bosch, August 19, 1952, JDC Archives Collection G45–54 Folder MO.76 Item 795412; Letter from Gonik to Acohen, August 21, 1952, JDC Archives Collection G45–54 Folder MO.76 Item 795409; Letter from Willink to Gonik, August 22, 1952, JDC Archives Collection G45–54 Folder MO.76 Item 795408.
50 Letter from Acohen to Gonik, September 25, 1952, attached to Letter from Gonik to Bein, September 30, 1952, JDC Archives Collection G45–54 Folder MO.76 Item 795398.
51 Letter from Health Department to AJDC Casablanca, November 7, 1952, JDC Archives Collection G45–54 Folder MO.78 Item 795634; Letter from Health Department to Raphael, December 31, 1952, JDC Archives Collection G45–54 Folder MO.78 Item 795532; Letter from Gonik to Bassewitz, January 19, 1952 [1953], JDC Archives Collection G45–54 Folder MO.77 Item 795528; Letter from A.J.D.C Casablanca to Shapiro, March 24, 1953, JDC Archives Collection G45–54 Folder MO.76 Item 795379; Letter from Neutraal Technisch Adviesbureau to American Joint Distribution Committee, July 30, 1952, JDC Archives Collection G45–54 Folder MO.77 Item 795483.
52 Letter from Supply Department to Health Department, July 18, 1952, JDC Archives Collection G45–54 Folder MO.77 Item 795511.
53 Letter from AJDC Paris to AJDC Casablanca, July 8, 1953, JDC Archives Collection G45–54 Folder MO.76 Item 795340.

Danish, and French infant formula companies that sent out information materials and formula samples.[54]

The question of where to place the milk plant in the dispensary was contested and highlighted the issue of capacities and workflows at the La Maternelle-OSE polyclinic. According to the plans, the milk station was to be installed in the basement of the building. This added yet another service to the already crowded setting, where also tinea and trachoma were treated. In fall 1952, Gonik approached the JDC headquarters with an idea for restructuring the current combination of health services, given his critical assessment of the inadequate workflows.[55] He proposed to relocate the tinea and trachoma service outside of the building of the La Maternelle-OSE dispensary and asked for a budget to build a temporary facility on a neighboring piece of land. Housing a pre-natal clinic, a well baby clinic, a sick baby clinic, and a milk station, it would make it possible to "consolidate" the Dispensaire La Maternelle-OSE "into an efficient maternal and childcare center."[56]

This plan was subject to discussion, reflecting the diverging visions of the future of the dispensary and the local institutional framework amongst the OSE-JDC management. Given the considerable technical effort of adapting the dispensary spaces for installing a milk-bottling plant, both Raphael and Bein proposed to instead set up the milk station in the envisioned new building. Besides the technical side of this idea, there was also a very concrete institutional interest. The building housing the La Maternelle-OSE dispensary actually belonged to the local Jewish aid society *La Maternelle* and not OSE-Morocco. Subsequently, "all the improvements put into the Maternelle will belong to the Maternelle," Bein wrote to Gonik – he advised "build[ing] our own building where we should be the 'bosses' and not the Maternelle."[57] This argument again highlights the occasionally strained cooperation between the various local and international Jewish relief actors on the ground. Gonik rejected this proposal, and emphasized that the new building was supposed to be only temporary because of the limited nature of the trachoma and tinea service, whereas the milk station was planned as "a fixed installation in a permanent building."[58] Unconvinced, Bein stressed the advan-

---

54 Memorandum from Levine to Gonik, July 2, 1953, JDC Archives Collection G45–54 Folder MO.76 Item 795334; Letter from AJDC Paris Budget Department to Raphael, July 2, 1953, JDC Archives Collection G45–54 Folder MO.76 Item 795338.
55 Memorandum from Health Department to Beckelman, September 15, 1952, 1, JDC Archives Collection G45–54 Folder MO.107 Item 796819.
56 Memorandum from Health Department to Beckelman, September 15, 1952, 3, JDC Archives Collection Folder MO.107 Item 796819.
57 Letter from Bein to Gonik, December 2, 1952, JDC Archives Collection G45–54 Folder MO.76 Item 795397.
58 Letter from Gonik to Bein, December 4, 1952, 1, JDC Archives Collection G45–54 Folder MO.76 Item 795396.

tages of his proposal, adding that the OSE offices could be relocated there as well: "Then OSE would be on the spot – nearer to the dispensary, nearer to the warehouse and nearer to the people."[59] However, Gonik stuck to the original plan.[60]

This debate amongst the JDC management showcases a diverging set of priorities: Bein emphasized the question of decision-making and streamlining the management of the JDC–OSE medical program in Casablanca. Gonik instead saw the matter as a question of conceptualizing the medical program in a coherent way. His vision for reorganization provides insights into the temporal dimension of the configuration of the healthcare program. Gonik understood the disease campaigns as a relatively manageable short-term endeavor, a notion rooted in contemporary ideas about "disease eradication." In contrast, the true core of the fight against poverty-related health issues and the long-term foundation of the aid activities was to be preventive maternal and child healthcare. Gonik won his point, and after that, the construction work for the milk station progressed without any major disruptions over the course of early spring 1953. At last, the milk station could fulfill its function as a prestige project. It became the epitome of the vision of effective aid and was promoted as such to attract further interest and support.

IV. Beyond Milk Bottles

The "model" milk station was more than a complicated negotiation between different stakeholders. It was also infused with a programmatic vision of raising a "healthy new generation" of Moroccan Jews, lifting them up from poverty and disease towards a productive future. The opening of the milk station hence functioned as a publicity event to showcase the concrete achievements and the feasibility of the overall program to past and future donors. Yet while initially conceived and presented as a core element of the maternal and child health program, the long-term value of the milk-bottling plant was soon called into question by the medical professionals involved.

Both the JDC and OSE relied on publicity to attract the donations that allowed them to pursue their programs. They repeatedly stressed the importance of

---

59 Letter from Bein to Gonik, December 8, 1952, 2, JDC Archives Collection G45–54 Folder MO.76 Item 795395. See also Letter from Raphael to A.J.D.C. Paris-Health Department, December 19, 1952, JDC Archives Collection G45–54 Folder MO.107 Item 796807; Letter from Raphael to Gonik, December 22, 1952, JDC Archives Collection G45–54 MO.76 Item 795393.
60 Letter from Health Department to Raphael, December 19, 1952, JDC Archives Collection G45–54 Folder MO.76 Item 795394; Letter from Health Department to AJDC-Casablanca, December 23, 1952, JDC Archives Collection G45–54 Folder MO.107 Item 796806.

"propaganda" aimed at partners and supporters and published a range of information material. Public events such as inaugurations, anniversaries, or openings served to demonstrate the responsible use of donations and funds and to convey a sense of the concrete achievements, accountability, and feasibility of the program. They were occasions to address potential donors and to seek out new contributions.[61] Inaugurations and official visits were regularly covered in the Moroccan and international Jewish press and featured prominently in the JDC's and OSE's publicity work. Photographs of the aid projects and of visitors inspecting the services circulated widely between the various organizations involved and were reused and reframed in different contexts.[62]

The inauguration event of the milk station attests to the meaning the JDC and OSE attributed to its publicity effect. When the ceremony was planned in spring 1953, the timing was supposed to ensure that the milk station would already be fully functioning but would retain its novelty value. The attendance of high-ranking guests from the Jewish community, the authorities, and partner organizations also played an important role. The date was set to accommodate the schedule of Director of the Protectorate Public Health Department Georges Sicault.[63] Although Sicault, Gonik and the UNAC delegate were ultimately unable to attend, the inauguration was still considered a publicity success by the JDC.[64] OSE-Union, however, deemed the center of attention misplaced: they even issued a short press statement "wishing to make clear" the central role of the Dutch OSE and the UNAC in initiating the milk station, granting the JDC the role of assembler.[65] Irritated, Bein wrote to Gonik that the JDC had actually "invested somewhat more labor than only a rectification in the press."[66] Here again, the

---

61 Johannes Paulmann (ed.), *Humanitarianism and Media: 1900 to the Present* (New York: Berghahn Books, 2018); Heide Fehrenbach and Davide Rodogno (eds.), *Humanitarian Photography: A History* (Cambridge: Cambridge University Press, 2015).
62 See also "Michal Ben Ya'akov Lectures on Images of Moroccan Jews and Perceptions of American Jews, 1942–1954," https://archives.jdc.org/michal-ben-yaakov-lectures-on-images-of-moroccan-jews/ (December 1, 2023).
63 Letter from Raphael to Sabah, April 22, 1953, JDC Archives Collection G45–54 Folder MO.76 Item 795368.
64 Letter from Bein to Katzki and Gonik, June 1, 1953, JDC Archives Collection G45–54 Folder MO.76 Item 795351; "La Biberonnerie de l'O.S.E., arme précieuse contre la mortalité infantile," JDC Archives Collection G45–54 Folder MO.76 Item 795353. The inauguration also featured prominently in a photo album assembled by OSE-Morocco and sent to the OSE office in the United States: "OSE Activities in Morocco," 1956, YIVO Archives RG 494 OSE Photograph Collection Folder 104 (Morocco2).
65 Extrait des Nouvelles Juives Mondiales No. J. 516, 9 Juin, "La Biberonnerie de Casablanca," JDC Archives Collection G45–54 Folder MO.76 Item 795342 [In French, quotation translated]. See also the respective press clipping, Coupures d'informations relatives à l'activité de l'OSE à travers le monde, CAHJP Collection Union Mondiale OSE Folder OSE-PAR-290.
66 Letter from Bein to Medical Department, June 22, 1953, JDC Archives Collection G45–54 Folder MO.76 Item 795341.

OSE-Union's view of a "takeover" by the JDC clashed with the JDC's self-understanding as the major driving force of any of these projects.

Shortly before the inauguration, in late April 1953 the milk station was visited by Leonard Heller, president of the United Jewish Fund and Council St. Paul, Minnesota, and himself a milk producer in Minneapolis. His visit paradigmatically shows how closely entangled infant feeding, the circulation of commodities from the United States and Europe to Morocco, the grander programmatic visions shared by American Jewish fundraising networks, and the publicity value attributed to the installation were. Bein, who regularly welcomed visitors and delegations, showed Heller and his wife the JDC program in Casablanca, and especially the milk station. He later emphasized the "most interesting coincidence" of such a visit "at the final stage" of building the milk station.[67] The visit also provided a welcome opportunity for publicity materials: As Bein reported, they photographed Heller in the role of an aid worker "distributing cups of milk to undernourished children in one of our centers." Another photo, "which is rather interesting, shows where in our warehouse we found some barrels of USDA milk actually originating from St. Paul, Minn., which is Mr. Heller's home town."[68] Overall, Bein expressed his confidence about having won valuable advocates in the United States.[69] He quoted a telegram by Heller, who lauded the "enthusiasm and resourcefulness of Joints [JDC, J.S.] staff here" and confirmed that "[e]very Dollar spent here does [the] work of four," thus affirming the efficiency of the program. According to Heller, this contributed to a grander societal vision, as it "will enable [a] whole generation of children doomed to incredible existence to grow to [sic] productive enlightened world citizens."[70]

This vision of individual and collective change for Moroccan Jewry towards an ideal of productiveness, enlightenment, and cosmopolitanism framed the milk station and the overall OSE-JDC medical program as a profoundly transformative endeavor. Heller's statement resonated well with JDC claims made at the inauguration. For example, the above-mentioned press release circulating in var-

---

67 Letter from AJDC Casablanca to Cohen, May 5, 1953, 1, JDC Archives Collection G45–54 Folder FR.595 Item 789298.
68 Letter from AJDC Casablanca to Cohen, May 5, 1953, 1, JDC Archives Collection G45–54 Folder FR.595 Item 789298. Copies of the photographs: NY_16877, NY_12863, NY_12862, NY_12861, JDC Archives Photograph Collection; umja0017.048.2.1, umja0017.048.2.2, umja0017.048.2.3, umja0017.048.2.4, University of Minnesota Libraries, Nathan and Theresa Berman Upper Midwest Jewish Archives, Sharron and Oren Steinfeldt Photography Collection.
69 Letter from AJDC Casablanca to Cohen, May 5, 1953, 2, JDC Archives Collection G45–54 Folder FR.595 Item 789298.
70 Telegram quoted in Letter from AJDC Casablanca to Cohen, May 6, 1953, JDC Archives Collection G45–54 Folder FR.595 Item 789297.

ious American Jewish newspapers highlighted the broader vision behind the JDC's medical program in Morocco regarding the children's future potential: "Give them a decent chance in life and, like children everywhere, they'll grow into useful and productive citizens – either of their native land or of Israel, where many hope one day to settle."[71] Of which nation, state, or society Moroccan Jews were to become citizens was an open question in a post-Holocaust world marked by decolonization.[72] That healthcare and milk supply for Moroccan Jews was infused with these transformative ideals testifies to the ways in which aid was a reciprocal relationship between donors, aid workers, and recipients.

After the long installation process had finally culminated in a successful inauguration and in positive publicity, the daily operation soon proved to be challenging in its own way. The contentious question which children were deemed in need of or entitled to receiving milk was subject to a continuous debate and sheds light on two blurred lines: the demarcation between milk as medicine or food, and the boundary between a medical and a social aid program. In the milk station's planning stage, the French Protectorate Public Health Department generally agreed to its installation on the condition "that biberons are only issued on strictly medical indications," an outlook that aligned well with OSE-Morocco's intentions, as Raphael confirmed at the time.[73] However, once the milk station was up and running, this line began to blur and "the number of bottles per child augmented out of proportion."[74] Raphael complained that dispensary doctors prescribed milk beyond medical indication. This was not only a problem in terms of potentially overstretching the French administration's permission but also in terms of straining the limited resources available.[75] The question of who should and would benefit from the produced milk remained an unresolved issue during the period in which the milk station operated.

While the facility initially had been deemed a success and a necessity for an adequate and modern preventive healthcare program, by the late 1950s this view changed. Only a couple of years after its inauguration, the discussion at the JDC and OSE-Morocco management level already revolved around the question of abolishing the plant due to increasing doubts about its efficacy. In late 1957, in now independent Morocco, newly appointed Medical Director M.P.D. Martin

---

71 "Milk-Bottling Plant for Children of Casa Mellah," JDC Archives Collection G45–54 Folder MO.76 Item 795352.
72 See also Mooreville, "Oculists in the Orient," 147.
73 Letter from Raphael to Union-OSE, September 22, 1950, 2, JDC Archives Collection G45–54 Folder MO.76 Item 795447.
74 Report on O.S.E.-Maroc, January 1954, 17, JDC Archives Collection G55–64 Folder ORG.521 Item 2879093.
75 Report on O.S.E.-Maroc, January 1954, 17–18, JDC Archives Collection G55–64 Folder ORG.521 Item 2879093.

raised the fundamental point: "To bi-beronnerie or not to bi-beronnerie, that is the question." Yet despite the growing costs he acknowledged the still valid "[p]ropaganda value of the biberonnerie when showing it ot [sic] authorities and visitors."[76] However, not only did maintenance, distribution, and expenses continue to be contested issues, but a conceptual shift also became apparent.

The education and active participation of the mothers started to gain higher priority in OSE-Morocco's program from the mid-1950s onwards, resonating with US and international models of public health and maternal and infant health. In the phase of building the plant, the JDC had sought out US public health experts for recommendations on the appropriate set-up of milk distribution centers. In general, the chief of the Child Development Research Branch of the Children's Bureau in Washington had agreed on the usefulness of milk stations, yet explained that in the United States, the current emphasis lay more on the "education of the mother rather than distribution of prepared feedings." When planning a milk station in "underdeveloped areas," she further explained that there was a "double problem": to install the facility in the most simple and inexpensive manner so the work could continue "when foreign support is withdrawn," and – given the delicacy of milk as a substance – to ensure the safety to prevent the milk station from doing "more harm than good."[77] This position points to a key question in the history of development: the applicability of models and strategies from one setting to another and how these concepts themselves were infused with temporalities. Whereas in the United States, the distribution of ready-made milk bottles may have become an outdated concept, Morocco was framed as a setting where such models might still be of use.

What in 1953 was considered a well-established and modern approach was now seen as anachronistic. While the cutting-edge technology had been celebrated at the inauguration, ten years later, in 1963, newly appointed OSE-Morocco Medical Director Fred Tavill professed that "the milk station program has accentuated the mechanical side of infant feeding to the neglect of the human element."[78] And since uninterrupted sterilization could not always be guaranteed, the distribution of milk bottles was increasingly seen as a potential health

---

76 OSE-Maroc Budget Proposal for 1958, Narrative Report by Dr. M.P.D. Martin [Undated], 22, JDC Archives Collection G55–64 Folder ORG.521 Item 2879090.
77 Letter from Crane to Cantor, July 24, 1952, 1, attached to Letter from Supply Department to Health Department, August 1, 1952, JDC Archives Collection G45–54 Folder MO.77 Item 795479. See also Katharine K. Merritt: "A Simplified Method of Preparing Infants' Formulas," December 4, 1950, JDC Archives Collection G45–54 Folder MO.77 Item 795470. The Children's Bureau of the US Department of Labor was rooted in pre-World War I progressivism. Gillespie, "International Organizations and the Problem of Child Health," 121–122; Packard, *A History of Global Health*, 97.
78 Highlights of the Health Program of OSE Morocco Condensed from a Report Prepared in July 1963 by Dr. F. Tavill, August 1963, 6, JDC Archives G55–64 Folder ORG.505 Item 2878980.

hazard.[79] After ten years of existence, the milk station was closed in August of that year.[80] This was not the end of milk, however. Nutrition and milk supply continued to play an important role in OSE-Morocco's medical program, albeit in a different form: in line with other health education formats, the demonstration of how to prepare meals and how to use milk powder took center stage in the JDC–OSE infant feeding program.[81] This resonated with international developments, as UNICEF's focus on milk powder was toned down over the course of the 1950s, due to both material and conceptual shifts.[82] The planning and opening of the milk station in the early 1950s thus proved to be a point of convergence that soon seemed to have outlived its purpose and feasibility when it came to reaching the programmatic goal of raising a "healthy new generation" of Moroccan Jews.

V. Conclusion

In the early 1950s, the plan to install a milk station to combat infant mortality amongst the impoverished Jewish community of Casablanca brought together humanitarian actors from a variety of backgrounds, linking postwar North Africa, Europe, and America. Along with other internationally operating Jewish organizations, the JDC and OSE developed a deep interest in the fate of Moroccan Jews in postwar Morocco, where the anticolonial independence movement put increasing pressure on French colonial rule. In the late 1940s, the founding of OSE-Morocco was a shared effort by leading Moroccan Jewish public figures, the OSE healthcare network, and the JDC. As part of broader community and international aid on behalf of Moroccan Jews, OSE-Morocco's program targeted children and mothers and sought to contribute to raising a "new generation" that would lead "productive" lives in Morocco or Israel. The milk station was one of these projects and expanded the existent medical services offered at the Casablanca polyclinic La Maternelle-OSE, at least for the ten years it was operational.

---

79 See for example, Proceedings of the Conference on Medical and Health Problems in Areas of AJDC Activity held at UNESCO House in Paris June 28th–July 1st, 1954, JDC Archives Collection G45–54 Folder SM.765 Item 2570776.
80 OSE-Maroc Rapport d'Activité 1963, 6, CAHJP Collection Union Mondiale OSE Folder OSE-PAR-69; Highlights of the Health Program of OSE Morocco Condensed from a Report Prepared in July 1963 by Dr. F. Tavill, August 1963, 6, JDC Archives G55–64 Folder ORG.505 Item 2878980; Transcript of Interview with Fred Tavill conducted by Herbert Katzki November 12, 1993, 35–36, JDC Archives Oral History Collection, Herbert Katzki Oral History Project 1974–2010 File 151.
81 Perry H. Haber: Report on Field Trip to Morocco for Consultation on Nutrition and Feeding Programs, April 29th to May 21st 1963, JDC Archives Collection G55–64 Folder MO.171 Item 2791266.
82 Gillespie, "International Organizations and the Problem of Child Health," 136–144.

Embedded in the postwar landscape of international bodies and transnational aid networks, the milk station project was a product of the continuous momentum of milk powder in emergency feeding programs and late colonial public health initiatives in the aftermath of World War II. Initially made possible by a donation from the Dutch UNAC committee, the protracted process of funding and installing the equipment for the milk-bottling plant showcased the frictions between European Jewish networks and the approaches of American Jewish aid organizations. The ways the conflict evolved and how it was solved shed light on the complex dynamics of inter-organizational cooperation and competition in the history of humanitarianism. Highlighting the reciprocal configuration of aid, the inauguration ceremony attested to the unbroken publicity value of the milk station and how prestige projects were used for validating the efficacy of aid programs and attracting future support.

In its dual role between food and medicine, the distribution of milk highlighted the blurred line between healthcare and social aid in Jewish medical humanitarianism for Moroccan Jews. With conceptual shifts away from handing out ready-made bottles of milk towards health education, the milk station, however, quickly outlived its appeal as a modern public health institution in the late 1950s, an evolution that was in in line with international developments in the field of milk supply. In the milk station project, a new sense of urgency by Jewish organizations, long-standing maternal and infant healthcare concepts, and postwar relief structures intersected. Overall, the milk station project epitomized broader currents in Jewish medical humanitarianism in late colonial Morocco and contested visions of Jewish futures in a postwar world marked by decolonization.

Sarah Knoll

Humanitarianism as a Policy Strategy? Revisiting Austria's 'Humanitarian Tradition'

"In keeping with its humanitarian tradition, Austria supports international efforts to ensure effective humanitarian aid in host countries and better care for Syrian refugees in the region." With these words, Foreign Minister Alexander Schallenberg (Austrian People's Party, ÖVP) justified the distribution of humanitarian funds totaling 2 million euros in 2019. The donations were intended to support Syrian refugees in Jordan, Lebanon, and Yemen.[1] In April 2023, in the wake of an armed conflict in the Sudan, Ewa Ernst-Dziedzic (The Green Party) and Reinhold Lopatka (ÖVP) highlighted Austria's humanitarian aid for the country by referring to Austria's past and tradition: "In keeping with its humanitarian tradition and in view of the worrying situation in Sudan, Austria has so far supported the humanitarian efforts of the international community in Sudan".[2] This narrative of Austria's humanitarian tradition is not a new one, however. During a 2010 discussion in the Austrian parliament on the right of asylum, Angela Lueger, a member of parliament for the Social Democratic Party (SPÖ), called on Austria's "very humanitarian tradition in the asylum system"[3] and stated that the country "has always fulfilled its obligations at a very high level." Willibald Pahr, crossbench foreign minister in a one-party government of the SPÖ, already highlighted at the General Assembly of the United Nation in 1982 that "Austria will not stop taking care of desperate people seeking help and considers it a moral obligation, an essential element of our humanitarian policy, to continue to be a haven of freedom and a source of hope despite economic

---

1 All translations from German to English are mine and edited by John Heath. Alexander Schallenberg: "Österreich setzt sein humanitäres Engagement konsequent fort," Bundesministerium für europäische und internationale Angelegenheiten, 11 September 2019, https://www.bmeia.gv.at/ministerium/presse/aktuelles/2019/09/alexander-schallenberg-oesterreich-setzt-sein-humanitaeres-engagement-konsequent-fort/ (21 February 2024).
2 Entschließungsantrag betreffend sofortige Einstellung der bewaffneten Auseinandersetzung im Sudan (3365/A(E)), eingebracht am 27 April 2023, https://www.parlament.gv.at/dokument/XXVII/A/3365/fnameorig_1555437.html (21 February 2024).
3 Nationalrat, XXIV. GP, 53. Sitzung 29. Jänner 2010, 232, https://www.parlament.gv.at/dokument/XXIV/NRSITZ/53/fname_181931.pdf (21 February 2024).

difficulties."[4] He framed his commitment to the vulnerable all over the world as a part of Austria's 'humanitarian foreign policy,' which focused on human rights, a tolerant refugee and asylum policy, and solidarity in the event of disasters.[5]

The list of statements by Austrian politicians on Austria's supposed humanitarian tradition and the country's humanitarian policy could be extended further. Most striking about the references to "Austria's humanitarian tradition" seems to be a cross-party political consensus over different periods of time. Moreover, not only Austria's politicians have time and again called on its humanitarian tradition, but both confessional and non-confessional non-governmental organizations (NGOs) have done – and still do – so. They often use this trope to remind the Austrian government about its commitment to people in need. For instance, in August 2023, Shoura Hashemi, the managing director of Amnesty International, called for a "revival of the humanitarian tradition that once existed in Austria," especially when it comes to asylum for refugees.[6] Hashemi was not alone. In April 2016, Caritas, an aid organization of the Roman Catholic Church, for example, warned that the then planned massive tightening of the asylum law was a departure from the country's humanitarian tradition.[7]

The narrative of Austria's "humanitarian tradition" therefore appears not only as a political catchword, but is also evoked as an inherent part of Austria's self-perception. Political and social actors have continuously demanded and portrayed it as a constitutive part of Austria's foreign policy. Humanitarian politics, standards, and motives seem to resonate with larger parts of the public sphere and society in Austria. What are the origins of the narrative of "humanitarian Austria," how has it evolved, and how has it related to international humanitarianism? This paper discusses these key questions.

Today, it seems common sense to understand humanitarianism as a non-political activity. This assumption is strongly connected with the Red Cross, its history, and its guiding principles of humanitarian aid: humanity, equality, proportionality, impartiality, neutrality, independence, and universality. As Joël Glasman has reconstructed, these principles were codified by International Committee of the Red Cross (ICRC) lawyer Jean Pictet as a reaction to the harsh criticism of the organization's ambivalent role during the Second World War and

---

4 Erklärung des Bundesministers für Auswärtige Angelegenheiten Dr. Willibald Pahr vor der 37. Generalversammlung der Vereinten Nationen am 28. September 1982, in *Außenpolitischer Bericht* 1988, edited by Bundesministerium für auswärtige Angelegenheiten (BMAA) (Vienna: BMAA, 1982), 255–261, 259.
5 Vorwort in *Außenpolitischer Bericht* 1979, edited by BMAA (Vienna: BMAA, 1979), 8.
6 Amnesty International appelliert an humanitäre Tradition, *orf.at*, 23. August 2023, https://orf.at/stories/3328483/ (21 February 2024).
7 Presseaussendung 27.4.2016, Massive Verschärfung des Asylrechts ist Abkehr von humanitärer Tradition, https://www.caritas.at/ueber-uns/news/detail/news/74526-massive-verschaerfung-des-asylrechts-ist-abkehr-von-humanitaerer-tradition/ (21 February 2024).

the Holocaust and the ICRC's claim to be the "guardian of humanitarian principles."[8] At the heart of this doctrine was "impartiality," which was nothing new for the Red Cross, as this principle had already been invented by Henry Dunant and the authors of the 1864 Geneva Convention. But in contrast to Henry Dunant, who defined "impartiality" as a way to overcome discrimination on the battlefield and to humanize warfare, Pictet had a more universal definition in mind and reacted to the global increase in the need for humanitarian aid during and after the Second World War. He combined the idea of "impartiality" with "equality" and "proportionality." The Red Cross principle of "impartiality" was adopted by almost all humanitarian organizations, such as Médecins Sans Frontières (MSF) or the United Nations High Commission for Refugees (UNHCR), and became an argument for these organizations' supposed "impartiality." Helping people in need is, however, always a political task and impacts the region where aid missions are carried out, as Joël Glassman again highlights.[9] Therefore, the depoliticization of humanitarian work neglects the connection between political power in humanitarian projects and the influence of the interests of the donors, especially states.[10] Which society in need was considered at a given time as "worthy" or "unworthy" of receiving a relief mission by donor societies has always been a political question too. Geopolitical constellations and available resources but also the interests of the involved actors, governments, and organizations have always determined these prioritizations.[11] As the State Department of the United States under Secretary Henry Kissinger (1923–2023) accurately highlighted in 1976, "disaster relief is increasingly becoming a major instrument of our foreign policy."[12]

---

8 Joël Glasman, *Humanitarianism and the Quantification of Human Needs. Minimal Humanity* (New York: Routledge, 2019); Joël Glasman, "The invention of impartiality: the history of a humanitarian principle, from a legal, strategic and algorithmic perspective," 18 November 2020, https://msf-crash.org/en/publications/invention-impartiality-history-humanitarian-principle-legal-strategic-and-algorithmic (22 June 2024).

9 Joël Glasman, "Die Politik aus dem Nirgendwo. Humanitäre Hilfe und die Geschichte schwereloser Institutionen," in *Geschichte der Gegenwart*, 22 November 2022, https://geschichtedergegenwart.ch/die-politik-aus-dem-nirgendwo-humanitaere-hilfe-und-die-geschichte-schwereloser-institutionen/ (22 June 2024).

10 Peter J. Hoffman and Thomas G. Weiss, *Humanitarianism, War, and Politics. Solferino to Syria and Beyond* (Lanham/Boulder/New York/London: Rowman & Littlefield, 2018), 4–6; Thomas G. Weiss, "Humanitarian Action," in *The Oxford Handbook of International Organizations*, edited by Jacob Katz Cogan, Ian Hurd, and Ian Johnstone (Oxford: University Press 2016), 2–4, DOI: 10.1093/law/9780199672202.003.0014.

11 Weiss, Humanitarian Action, 2; Travis Nelson, "Humanitarian Motivations," in *The Routledge Companion to Humanitarian Action*, edited by Roger Mac Ginty and Jenny H Peterson (London–New York: Routledge, 2015), 74–84.

12 Cit. from Michael Barnett, "Compassion and Humanitarianism in International Relations," in *The Cambridge History of America and the World*, edited by David C. Engerman, Max Paul Friedman, and Melani McAlister (Cambridge: University Press, 2022), 349–369, 350.

Moreover, today humanitarian aid is understood as more than emergency relief but also includes long-term technical assistance. What started as relief work in wartime in 1864 already changed following the foundation of the *League of Red Cross Societies* (LORCS) in 1919. LORCS expanded humanitarian activities towards natural disasters and health emergencies in peacetime. Before the Second World War, humanitarian relief was already intertwined with regional development projects, as Davide Rodogno shows for the Near East.[13] This complex connection between humanitarian, reconstruction, and development aid continued during the postwar years and the Cold War. The foundation of the United Nations Industrial Development Organization (UNIDO) in 1966 marked a milestone in the institutionalization process of development aid, and serves here as example of the growing entanglements between technical support, development, and humanitarian ideas in the first United Nations Decade of Development (1960–1970).[14]

But political consideration not only shaped where relief funding is distributed. Humanitarian aid offered by states also serves a purpose in domestic politics, such as creating narratives about a state's and – by extension – a society's identity. This is what has happened in Austria. Ever since the reestablishment of state sovereignty and the commitment to neutrality in 1955, the self-portrayal as a humanitarian country made humanitarianism an immanent part of Austria's identity. Consequently, humanitarian aid offered by Austria has not only had an external effect on the recipients but also an internal impact, becoming a powerful narrative during the nation building process after the Second World War. The idea of humanitarian support was combined with questions of international prestige and visibility, the country's ties to the 'West,' neutrality, and state security.

In doing so, the Austrian government relied not only on the distribution of aid supplies but also on the settlement of international humanitarian organizations within the country's borders. The governments of the Second Republic understood the presence of international organizations as a means of positioning Austria on the stage of international diplomacy and relations. But it was also an opportunity to provide Austrian society with the presence of actors that mirrored claims to be perceived as a 'Western'-oriented place of dialogue. This strategy targeted not only agencies with health agendas but also agencies that focused more on development cooperation or technical support. Against this backdrop,

---

13 Davide Rodogno, *Night on Earth. A History of International Humanitarianism in the Near East, 1918–1930* (Cambridge: University Press, 2021).
14 For the connection between humanitarianism and development see Corrinna Unger, *International Development: A Postwar History* (London: Bloomsbury Academic, 2018); Agnieszka Sobocinska, *Saving the world? Western volunteers and the rise of the humanitarian-development complex* (Cambridge: University Press 2021).

the establishment of the UNIDO headquarters in Vienna in 1967 can be understood as an important success in the country's strategy of establishing Vienna as a location for international organizations and as a way to strengthen Austria's humanitarian stance.[15] The establishment of the headquarters of the International Atom Energy Agency (IAEA) in 1956 and of UNIDO led to the creation of the so-called UNO-City in Vienna.[16] Roughly ten years later, in 1979, Vienna was considered the third headquarters of the United Nations alongside New York and Geneva.[17]

This paper analyses the question of how humanitarianism has been used as a political strategy by the Austrian government. How has humanitarian support shaped Austria's identity? What goals has the government associated with humanitarian aid and hosting humanitarian organizations? To this end, the paper traces three levels. First, it looks at the initial founding moments and the construction of the narrative of 'humanitarian Austria' with a focus on domestic politics. Second, it focuses on Austria's humanitarian attitude as a way of legitimizing the country's independence and connection to the 'West' on a foreign policy level. And third, it traces the fine line between humanitarian promises and their implementation. Therefore, examples of where Austrian government's humanitarian claims are at odds with *realpolitik* are analyzed to illustrate how the humanitarian tradition worked in practice. The analysis is organized around two key moments: the 'Hungarian refugee crisis,' which took place in autumn 1956 and played a crucial role in Austria's identity-building process, and another key moment in the process of strengthening Austria's positive international perception, the idea of attracting international humanitarian organizations to set up headquarters in Austria, which began in 1956. This was a major political step towards gaining international visibility and trustworthiness.

This paper thus examines the beginning of Austria's self-perception as a humanitarian country, which began in neighboring Hungary, and then analyses the construction of the UNO-City as one consequence of this humanitarian state identity. Both events are crucial for an understanding of Austria's humanitarian tradition.

---

15 For the connection of development policies, humanitarian ideas, and states interests in Austria, see Lucile Dreidemy, *Internationale Politik ohne staatliche Akteure? Das Wiener Institut für Entwicklungsfragen und die sozialdemokratischen Nord-Süd-Netzwerke im globalen Kalten Krieg*, Habilitationsschrift, University of Vienna 2023.

16 Sarah Knoll and Elisabeth Röhrlich, "Das neutrale Österreich als Sitz internationaler Organisationen: Entstehung und Verselbständigung politischer Narrative," in *Österreichischen Zeitschrift für Politikwissenschaft* 53 (2024), DOI 10.15203/4185.vol53.2024.

17 Since 1996, a fourth headquarters of the United Nations has been located in Nairobi, Kenya.

I. Hungary 1956: the founding moment of a narrative

In autumn 1956, the influx of about 180,000 refugees from Hungary following the Hungarian revolution marked a political and humanitarian crisis in Austria,[18] but also gave the government under chancellor Julius Raab (ÖVP) the opportunity to shape Austria's independent and neutral role in the world by helping refugees. As Karin Liebhart and Andreas Pribersky point out, humanitarian aid became an important part of the Second Republic's identity as a consequence of the Hungarian Revolution of 1956.[19]

From autumn 1956 onwards, Hungarian citizens openly called for an end to the one-party rule of the Hungarian Working People's Party and for democratization. The protests, initially carried out mostly by students, culminated in a revolution against the ruling communist system in October 1956. Driven by the demonstrations, the acting prime minister of Hungary, Imre Nagy (1896–1958), announced the formation of a coalition government and Hungary's unilateral withdrawal from the Warsaw Pact, declared the country's neutrality, and requested the United Nations for help. All hopes for political change were crushed on 4 November 1956, when the invasion of the Soviet army suppressed the protests.[20]

The consequence was the movement of refugees to Austria, who reached the country during a phase of political reorganization after the end of the Second World War. Just a year earlier, Austria had restored its state sovereignty with the ratification of the State Treaty and adoption of the Neutrality Law.[21] The Neutrality Law in particular gained high political significance, as it laid the groundwork for Austria's general image of being a neutral country. Nevertheless, this law contained two articles that left room for interpretation. The law explicitly excluded the option of joining a military alliance (article 2). Furthermore, in article 1 Austria committed itself to "perpetual neutrality" ("immerwährende Neutralität") to secure its independence and declared it would "maintain and defend this neutrality with all means."[22] The commitment to neutrality, which had been a main goal of Austria's foreign policy since 1946/47, did not stop

---

18 Ibolya Murber, "Ungarnflüchtlinge in Österreich 1956," in *Die ungarische Revolution und Österreich 1956*, edited by Ibolya Murber and Zoltán Fónagy (Vienna: Czernin, 2006), 335–385, 336.
19 Karin Liebhart and Andreas Pribersky, "Brücke oder Bollwerk? Grenzland Österreich–Ungarn," in *Memoria Austriae II. Bauten, Orte, Regionen*, edited by Emil Brix, Ernst Bruckmüller and Hannes Stekl (Vienna: Verlag für Geschichte und Politik, 2005), 411–441, 413–416.
20 György Dalos, *1956. Der Aufstand in Ungarn* (Munich: C.H.Beck, 2006).
21 Gerald Stourzh and Wolfgang Mueller, *Der Kampf um den Staatsvertrag 1945–1955: Ost-West-Besetzung, Staatsvertrag und Neutralität Österreichs* (Vienna–Cologne–Weimar: Böhlau, 2020).
22 Bundesgesetzblatt (BGBl.) 211/1955, Bundesverfassungsgesetz: Neutralität Österreich.

Austria from joining the United Nations as early as late 1955. Austria's 1947 application had been rejected due to discussions about its status as an enemy state during the Second World War. Official admission was not granted until December 1955, after the State Treaty.[23] Returning to the political stage via the United Nations had been a goal that all parties committed to after 1945. And, as Oliver Rathkolb has highlighted, membership of the United Nations was initially more important than joining the European Council.[24]

Hence the Hungarian revolution just a year later became the first real testing ground for Austria's declared neutrality and, moreover, offered numerous reference points for shaping Austria's postwar identity as progressive and a 'Western state.' It was an opportunity to fill 'neutrality' with meaning and define political strategies as well as creating a post-World-War II humanitarianism. These strategies had repercussions both internationally and internally.

From the very beginning of the uprising in Hungary, the Austrian government made no secret of its sympathy with the protesting Hungarian people.[25] It even appealed publicly to the Soviet Union to stop military action in Hungary and reestablish freedom and human rights.[26] Although the Austrian government feared negative consequences from the Soviet Union, Moscow paid little attention to the statement. The reception in the 'West' was much more positive. This marked the first step towards Austria's foreign self-presentation's taking shape as a humanitarian, peaceful, and democratic country.[27] Not only Austrian politicians responded to the situation; the nation's public did too. Sympathy for the protesting Hungarians had roots in anti-communist or anti-Soviet resentment due to Austria's experiences during the Soviet occupation, which had only ended a year earlier, and the persistence of National Socialist propaganda against communism.[28]

---

23 Erwin A. Schmidl, "Wien als internationales Zentrum," in *Wien seit 1945 – Die Metamorphose einer Stadt,* edited by Michael Dippelreiter (Vienna: Böhlau, 2013), 703–730, 705–707.
24 Oliver Rathkolb, *Die paradoxe Republik: Österreich 1945–2015* (Vienna: Zsolnay, 2015), 293–294.
25 Peter Haslinger, "Flüchtlingskrise 1956–die ungarische Revolution und Österreich," in "1956. (Nieco) inne spojrzenie. Eine (etwas) andere Perspektive," edited by Jerzy Kochanowski and Joachim von Puttkamer (Warsaw: Wydawnictwo Neriton, 2016), 125–156, 130.
26 Ministerratsprotokoll (MRP) Nr. 12a, 28 October 1956, Beilage A, Österreichische Staatsarchiv (ÖStA), Archiv der Republik (AdR), Bundeskanzleramt (BKA), MRP, 2. Republik, Raab II, Box 148.
27 Andreas Gémes, *Austria and the 1956 Hungarian Revolution. Between Solidarity and Neutrality* (Pisa: University Press, 2008), 26–28.
28 Elisabeth Röhrlich, *Kreiskys Außenpolitik. Zwischen österreichischer Identität und internationalem Programm* (Vienna: University Press, 2009), 127 f.; Rathkolb, *Paradoxe Republik*, 33; Franz Cede and Christian Prosl, *Anspruch und Wirklichkeit: Österreichs Außenpolitik seit 1945* (Innsbruck/Vienna/Bolzano, 2015), 33.

However, the narrative of 'humanitarian Austria' became most palpable when the federal government launched a campaign supporting the Hungarian refugees. As historian Manfried Rauchensteiner puts it: "It was not tanks and soldiers that measured the readiness to defend freedom, but the tons of relief supplies and the millions in donations."[29] On 28 October 1956, the government decided to provide accommodation for around 10,000 refugees in the country and acted generously by granting asylum. The Council of Ministers (Ministerrat) even decided that every person fleeing Hungary was granted the right of asylum, irrespective of their motives for leaving the country.[30] This decision was not revised even when the government started to realize in mid-November 1956 that Hungarians also fled for more pragmatic reasons than for political ones.[31]

The decision to act 'generously' was driven more by foreign interests than by an impulse of charitable benevolence. First, Austria wanted to be seen as part of the 'West' but without starting a conflict with the Soviet Union over neutrality.[32] The government thus presented the help for refugees as humanitarian and an act of charity. To avoid accusations of partiality and due to financial and structural needs, the Austrian government mandated local and international relief organization to coordinate the relief mission.[33] Second, the 'Hungarian refugee crisis' created a window of opportunity to establish a new and positive picture of the Austria in the world which stood in contrast to the National Socialist past. Although until the late 1980s Austria's post-war history was based on the victim narrative, which presented the country as the first victim of the National Socialism aggression with the "Anschluss" on 12 March 1938,[34] Austria's participation in the crimes of the National Socialist regime remained a fact, which made consolidating values of humanity all the more necessary as a counter-image. As a consequence, ever since its birth in 1956, Austria's narrative of

---

29 Manfried Rauchensteiner, *Spätherbst 1956. Die Neutralität auf dem Prüfstand* (Vienna: Österreichischer Bundesverlag, 1981), 67.
30 MRP Nr. 12a, 28 October 1956, ÖStA, AdR, BKA, MRP, 2. Republik, Raab II, Box 148; Patrik-Paul Volf, "Der politische Flüchtling als Symbol der Zweiten Republik. Zur Asyl- und Flüchtlingspolitik seit 1945," *zeitgeschichte* 22 (1995) 11–12: 415–435, 430.
31 MRP Nr. 15, 13 November 1956, ÖStA, AdR, BKA, MRP, 2. Republik, Raab II, Box 148; Ibolya Murber, "Die Betreuung und Integration von Ungarnflüchtlingen in Österreich 1956/57," in *Migration–Flucht–Vertreibung–Integration*, edited by Stefan Karner and Barbara Stelzl-Marx (Graz–Vienna: Lykam, 2019), 103–120, 108 f.
32 Liebhart and Pribersky, "Brücke oder Bollwerk," 413–416; Volf, "politische Flüchtling," 429 f.
33 Sarah Knoll, "Calling for Support. International aid for refugees in Austria during the Cold War," *zeitgeschichte* 48 (2021) 3, 387–408, 395–399.
34 The Moscow Declaration of 1943 legitimized this victim narrative. Only discussions starting in 1986 about the National Socialist past of president candidate Kurt Waldheim led to Austria being recognized as a country of perpetrators. Rathkolb, *Paradoxe Republik*, 50 f.; Manfried Rauchensteiner, *Unter Beobachtung. Österreich seit 1918* (Vienna–Cologne–Weimar: Böhlau, 2017), 221–225.

humanitarianism was infused by the country's experiences during the Second World War, but framed by the perspective of being its first victim. Because of the "painful experience, which forced many Austrians to emigrate, Austria has a special obligation to grant asylum to refugees and emigrants regardless of their nationality, religion, or political convictions."[35] Austria's part in the expulsion and murder of Jews, Roma and Sinti, and political opponents during the National Socialism regime was intentionally omitted from this story.

The government's strategy was readily supported by Austria's media, which contributed to creating an image of Austrians as humanitarian and benevolent. Supported by the dichotomy of the Cold War and a pronounced anti-communist attitude, the media also underlined the country's connection to the 'West' in order to improve its international reputation.[36] A main reference used by politics and media alike was the support of the local Austrian community. In 1959, Friedrich Kern praised the patience and willingness of the Austrian population to donate.[37] *Bürgenländische Freiheit*, a local Social Democratic newspaper in the Burgenland, the federal province bordering Hungary, celebrated the extraordinary willingness of the province's people to donate and support Hungarians on their road to freedom. "A wall of humanity. The border community in the service of charity," read the headline.[38] An educational center that was converted into a refugee home was called a "bastion of freedom," and the "true humanity" of the volunteers involved was emphasized.[39]

This extraordinary willingness to help Hungarian refugees in the first few days and weeks soon became a narrative of glorification to which the politicians and the public reverted in similar situations. Confronted with the refugees from the German Democratic Republic (GDR) in 1989, the local population of the Burgenland fondly recalled the way they had helped Hungarian refugees thirty-three years earlier. "The Burgenländer are helping as they did in 1956," was the general tenor according to local newspapers.[40] To this day, the support for Hungarian refugees in 1956 is perceived as proof of Austria's humanitarian stance, although historians in particular challenge the narrative of the Austrian population's unlimited help for Hungarians.[41] As Brigitte Zierer reconstructs, from early 1957,

---

35   Bundespressedienst (ed.), Österreich als Asylland, Vienna 1981, 5.
36   Brigitta Zierer, "Willkommen Ungarnflüchtlinge 1956?," in *Asylland wider Willen: Flüchtlinge in Österreich im europäischen Kontext seit 1914*, edited by Oliver Ratholb and Gernot Heiss (Vienna: J & V, 1995), 157–172, 170.
37   Friedrich Kern, *Österreich. Offene Grenzen der Menschlichkeit: Die Bewältigung des ungarischen Flüchtlingsproblems im Geiste internationaler Solidarität* (Vienna: BMI, 1959), 11.
38   Ein Wall der Menschlichkeit, *Burgenländische Freiheit*, 25 November 1956, 3.
39   Eine Bastion der Freiheit, *Burgenländische Freiheit*, 16. Dezember 1956, 3.
40   Fast wie 1956. Die Welt schaut auf uns, *BF-Die Burgenland Woche*, 23 August 1989, 1–4, 2.
41   Béla Rasky, "'Flüchtlinge haben auch Pflichten'. Österreich und die Ungarnflüchtlinge 1956," Kakanien revisited, 1 October 2001, www.kakanien-revisited.at/beitr/fallstudie/BRasky1.pdf

the image of the heroic Hungarian 'freedom fighters' was gradually replaced in the public's perception of Hungarians as 'ungrateful economic migrants.'[42]

Nevertheless, the international tailwind was largely responsible for consolidating the narrative of 'humanitarian Austria.' Especially international organizations active in Austria in 1956, such as UNHCR, praised the Austrian government and people for their willingness to take in and provide aid to Hungarians. For example, James N. Read, deputy high commissioner for refugees, constantly highlighted Austria's generous attitude and "liberal manner" when it came to granting asylum to Hungarians.[43] The UNHCR report about Hungarian refugees in Austria pointed to the "very considerable effort" that the Austrian government made for Hungarian refugees in cooperation with various voluntary organizations.[44] In this way, humanitarian actors themselves served as agents for shaping Austria's 'humanitarian traditions.' The international community also praised Austria's "generosity,"[45] as the Belgian government put it, although the Austrian government constantly asked for resettlement opportunities and financial support.[46]

Through the Hungarian revolution and the support for refugees in 1956, the Austrian government connected the country's neutrality with humanitarian support. The positive international reputation that Austria gained paved the way for integrating values like humanity and freedom into a new national self-understanding. Helping people in need and being an asylum country became an inherent part of Austria's self-perception. In an interview, former president Rudolf Kirchschläger confirmed the importance of the 'Hungarian refugee crises' for Austria's state- and nation-building domestically and internationally: "Through the Hungarian Revolution, through our strong humanitarian commitment, through our generous right to asylum […]: It was really only this way that we began to gain a profile in the West [and] in the rest of the world of states

---

(22 February 2024); Zierer, "Willkommen Ungarnflüchtlinge"; Sarah Knolll, "Flucht über den 'Eisernen Vorgang'. Das Burgenland als Erstaufnahmeland im Kalten Krieg," *Geschichte und Region/Storia e Regione* 30 (2021) 2: 41–62.

42 Zierer, "Willkommen Ungarnflüchtlinge,"169f.
43 Telegrams from James N. Read, reprinted in W. Ḥallam Tuck and Carl A. Hardigg, Report On Survey of Hungarian Refugee Relief Problems in Austria, 15 January 1957 found in UNOG Library Geneva.
44 UNREF Executive Committee 4th Session, The Problem of Hungarian Refugees in Austria. An Assessment of the Needs and Recommendations for Future Actions (Submitted by the High Commissioner), United Nations, General Assembly, A/AC.79/49, 17 January 1957, 1.
45 Ereignisse in Ungarn, Demarche bei belgischer Regierung wegen Flüchtlingshilfe, 26. November 1956, ÖStA, AdR, BKA/AA, Sektion II-pol, 1956, Ungarn (3d GZl.551.190 Zl. 791.000–791.999), Box 404.
46 For the numerous offers of support, see ÖStA, AdR, BKA/AA, Sektion II-pol, 1956, Ungarn (3d GZl.551.190 Zl. 791.000–791.999), Box 404.

[...]."⁴⁷ Indeed, the positive international perception of Austria's support for Hungarian refugees was important for gaining international prestige.

This positive reputation concerned the two major parties at this time, the SPÖ and the ÖVP, which also formed a coalition. The overall goal of both parties was to present Austria as an independent, trustworthy, and useful 'Western' European state. As the then state secretary Bruno Kreisky (SPÖ) emphasized in 1956: "Just as the Red Cross is deeply connected to Switzerland, Austria must prove itself to the world as a country that grants asylum."⁴⁸

II. International organizations as foreign policy strategies

Offering help to refugees as it occurred during the 'Hungarian refugee crisis' was not the only strategy for gaining international prestige and promoting a new positive image of Austria as a progressive, democratic, and neutral state. In fact, the Austrian government used different strategies to bolster this narrative and make it sustainable. From the 1950s, the government also relied on international organizations setting up their headquarters in Austria. Although not intended as a humanitarian act by the Austrian government in the first instance, hosting international organizations underlined Austria's commitment to values of freedom and democracy and, moreover, connected the country to international humanitarian projects and peace initiatives. Furthermore, it helped the country gain a seat at the table of international politics.

As the government pointed out in 1979 during the inauguration of the United Nations headquarters in Vienna, Austria should function as a "place of encounter, dialogue and understanding."⁴⁹ Similar to the support for refugees, hosting international organizations served as an opportunity to disseminate a positive image of Austria in the world which broke with its National Socialist past. From the perspective of state-building, the commitment to hosting international organizations and conferences, especially the United Nations headquarters, today also known as the UNO-City, tightened Austria's bonds with the international arena. Nevertheless, it is important to emphasize that the reasons for investing in hosting international organizations were diverse and cannot be explained solely by state neutrality and international visibility. They ranged from claiming an active policy of neutrality to security concerns, to economic interests, and to attracting tourism. As in the case of the Hungarian refugees, it is important to

---

47 Cit. from Liebhart and Pribersky, "Brücke oder Bollwerk," 413.
48 Bruno Kreisky, *Im Strom der Politik. Erfahrungen eines Europäers* (Berlin: Goldmann, 1988), 231.
49 Österreich: Ort der Begegnung Vorwort in *Außenpolitischer Bericht 1979*, edited by BMAA (Vienna: BMAA, 1979), 180; see also Röhrlich, *Kreiskys Außenpolitik*, 276–282.

highlight that the SPÖ and the ÖVP again agreed on the political necessity of setting up the headquarters of international organizations in Austria.⁵⁰

With respect to hosting international organizations too, the year 1956 was also a key moment. The establishment of the headquarters of the International Atomic Energy Agency (IAEA) played a central role here. During discussions about its establishment, Vienna had already been mentioned as a possible site. As Elisabeth Röhrlich has meticulously reconstructed, Austrian politicians reacted enthusiastically when they heard Vienna had been considered. As in the case of the support for Hungarian refugees, Austria's international visibility was at the center of interest. Austrian diplomats lobbied passionately to bring IAEA to Vienna. Having IAEA based in Vienna would further define Austria's place in international relations. Austria's diplomats, like ambassador Franz Matsch, highlighted Vienna's "atmosphere of tolerance and respect for other people's point of view" and hence its suitability for establishing the IAEA headquarter in Vienna. In autumn 1956, the diplomats even thought that the support for Hungarian refugees would move the Soviet Union to withdraw its support for Vienna.⁵¹ However, this did not happen, and, as the first major international organization, the IAEA set up its headquarters in Vienna in 1957. Even though UNHCR had already moved an office to Vienna in 1951,⁵² the relocation of the IAEA was a pivotal moment that established international organizations as part of a foreign policy strategy after state sovereignty had been regained in 1955. The headquarter agreement between Austria and IAEA thus included certain privileges, such as tax-free shopping in the commissary shop and tax privileges for IAEA employees.⁵³ Such benefits were intended to serve as incentives for other organizations to set up their headquarters in Austria.⁵⁴

---

50 MRP Nr. 7, 7 June 1966, Vortrag an den Minsterrat, Ministerkomitee für die Etablierung weiterer internationaler Organisationen in Wien, ÖStA, AdR, BKA, MRP, 2. Republik, Klaus II, Box 244; MRP Nr. 27, 2 December 1966, Beilage F, BMAA Wahl Wiens zum Amtssitz der neuerrichteten UN-Organisation für Industrielle Entwicklung UNIDO genannt, ÖStA, AdR, BKA, MRP, 2. Republik, Klaus II, Box 251; Röhrlich, *Kreiskys Außenpolitik*, 276–278; Eric Frey, "Konferenzplatz Wien: Vienna as an International Conference Site," *Contemporary Austrian Studies* (Global Austria: Austria's Place in Europe and in the World) 2011, 147–160, 150–153.
51 Elisabeth Roehrlich, *Inspectors for peace: a history of the International Atomic Energy Agency*, Johns Hopkins nuclear history and contemporary affairs (Baltimore: Johns Hopkins University Press, 2022), 64–68, quote 65.
52 Lukas Schemper, "Der Hohe Flüchtlingskommissar der Vereinten Nationen, Österreich und Repatriierung sowjetischer Flüchtlinge," in *Österreich im Kalten Krieg: neue Forschungen im internationalen Kontext*, edited by Maximilian Graf and Agnes Meisinger (Vienna: University Press, 2016), 49–71.
53 BGBl. 82/1958, Abkommen zwischen der Republik Österreich und der Internationalen Atomenergie-Organisation über den Amtssitz der Internationalen Atomenergie-Organisation.
54 Knoll/Röhrlich, "Das neutrale Österreich."

The political interest in becoming the home of international organizations continued after 1956 and the establishment of the IAEA. In May 1965, the Austrian government – now a coalition between the ÖVP and the SPÖ under Josef Klaus (ÖVP) – discussed the conditions for attracting more international organizations to the country. In particular, the lack of an adequate congress center where United Nations meetings could be held was identified as a shortcoming.[55] The Council of Ministers set up a working group to examine the situation and come up with measures to attract new organizations and international conferences. This group included the Ministry of Trade and Reconstruction, the Ministry of Foreign Affairs, and representatives of the provincial governments of Vienna and Lower Austria.[56] Soon after the Austrian government decided to work on the conditions for hosting international organizations, the General Assembly of the United Nations in New York officially set up UNIDO on 17 November 1966.[57] The official foundation marked the end of a controversial discussion about establishing a new UN organization that would focus on industrial development.[58] UNIDO's missions targeted so-called developing countries, which, in the 1960s, were often also newly independent states following the decolonization that took place after the Second World War. In line with the ambition of the United Nations to address economic and social inequality in the world, the General Assembly recognized that "the industrialization of developing countries is essential for their economic and social development and for the expansion and diversification of their trade." The main purpose of UNIDO was thus to promote industrial development. Their projects included disseminating information on technology and industrialization, training skilled workers, helping governments establish industrial development programs, and finding external financing for specific industrial projects.[59] First and foremost, UNIDO was intended to serve as an exchange platform for knowledge on industrial development. This task was, however, intimately linked to the idea of humanitarianism. The overall goal was to work against poverty, inequality, and associated social and environmental maladies like hunger.[60] Hence even today UNIDO presents itself as a humanitarian actor and focuses on the vision of a "world without poverty and hunger,

---

55 MRP, Nr. 44, 4 May 1965, ÖStA, AdR, BKA, MRP, 2. Republik, Klaus I, Box 231.
56 MRP Nr. 7, 7 June 1966, Vortrag an den Mininisterrat, Ministerkomitee für die Etablierung weiterer internationaler Organisationen in Wien, ÖStA, AdR, BKA, MRP, 2. Republik, Klaus II, Box 244.
57 United Nations General Assembly, Resolution 2152 (XXI), United Nations Industrial Development Organization, 17 November 1966.
58 Daniel A. Holly, *L'ONUDI: l'Organisation des Nations unies pour le développement industriel, 1967-1995* (Paris: L'Harmattan, 1999), 19–60.
59 United Nations General Assembly, Resolution 2152 (XXI), United Nations Industrial Development Organization, 17 November 1966.
60 UNIDO (ed.), *The intellectual history of UNIDO* (UNIDO, 2016), 3.

where industry drives low-emission economies, improves living standards, and preserves the livable environment for present and future generations, leaving no one behind."[61]

During the founding process of UNIDO, the office of the Secretary-General of the United Nations was already searching for potential cities to host the organization. This search overlapped with the development of Austria's political strategy of bringing international organizations to the country. It was not surprising that Vienna showed interest in hosting UNIDO, as it combined the location of an international organization with foreign and domestic political interests in boosting the country's humanitarian tradition through an organization which perceives itself as an humanitarian actor. On 12 October 1966, the Austrian Permanent Mission to the United Nations in New York communicated the decision of the Austrian government to offer its capital as the location for the UNIDO headquarters. In its application letter to the United Nations, Austria's government highlighted its "genuine interest in the success of this United Nations activity." The country's neutrality was mentioned as one of the main reason why the country would be a suitable candidate for hosting UNIDO. Moreover, the government also pointed to a high degree of industrialization, which could make an important contribution to the industrialization of developing countries.[62]

However, the Austrian government also saw an opportunity to generate benefits for the country's domestic economy through the cooperation of local firms such as VOEST with UNIDO.[63] To that end, the government was interested in presenting an attractive offer to the UN. The benefits for UNIDO ranged from tax relief for employees to favorable pension and social security arrangements.[64] But in particular, Austria's willingness to finance the entire construction of the new United Nation headquarters in Vienna and to host both UNIDO and IAEA in new buildings[65] was regarded positively by the United Nations General Secre-

---

61 Our mandate, our vision, our work, https://www.unido.org/about-us/who-we-are (22 February 2024).
62 United Nations General Assembly, A/6468, Activities in the field of Industrial development, Austrian permanent mission to the United Nations, New York, 12 October 1966.
63 MRP Nr. 27, 2 December 1966, Beilage F, BMAA Wahl Wiens zum Amtssitz der neuerrichteten UN-Organisation für Industrielle Entwicklung UNIDO genannt, ÖStA, AdR, BKA, MRP, 2. Republik, Klaus II, Box 251.
64 BGBl. 245/1967, Abkommen zwischen der Republik Österreich und den Vereinten Nationen über den Amtssitz der Organisation der Vereinte Nationen für Industrielle Entwicklung samt Notenwechsel.
65 Vortrag an den Ministerrat, Errichtung eines definitiven Amtssitzes der UNIDO und der IAEO im Rahmen eines UN-Zentrums, Vienna, 21 February 1967, ÖStA, AdR, BKA, Verfassungsdienst (VD), VD/S 6/5 R 85, 670.233, Box 152; Dieter Lautner, "Die UNO-City in Wien. Loseblattsammlung," *Österreich Edition*, edited by the Austrian State Archives, 2022.

tariat.⁶⁶ To increase its foreign prestige, the Austrian government was willing to invest a lot of money to host UNIDO. In December 1966, the government already understood that the settlement of a United Nations organization would be an expensive task but that it was a price both coalition partners were willing to pay. The fact that Austria was ultimately able to prevail against Athens, Istanbul, Nairobi, Geneva, New York, and Paris in the elections for UNIDO's headquarters was, moreover, due to Austria's massive lobbying activities towards the member states of the United Nations.⁶⁷ Through bilateral negotiations they were eventually successful and in 1967 Vienna became the city of UNIDO's headquarters. All these negotiations and state interests were not officially communicated. To this day, the Austrian public perceives neutrality as the main reason that UNIDO and the United Nations established its headquarters in Vienna.⁶⁸

In 1979, the United Nations Headquarters in Vienna was finally inaugurated. In addition to UNIDO and the IAEA, other United Nations offices and units were transferred to Vienna to make full use of the new buildings. During its construction it quickly became clear that the buildings were too large for the requirements of UNIDO and IAEA. The Austrian government thus tried to bring other United Organizations to Vienna.⁶⁹ Today, in addition to UNIDO and IAEA, the United Nations Office in Vienna hosts an UNHCR office, the United Nations Office on Drugs and Crime (UNODC), the office for Outer Space Affairs, and the United Nations Office for Disarmament Affairs.⁷⁰ In 1978 the headquarters of the United Nations Relief and Works Agency for Palestine Refugees in the Near East (UNRWA) was transferred from Beirut to Vienna due to the Lebanese Civil War. UNRWA stayed in the city until 1997, when it moved to Gaza City as result of the Oslo Accords.⁷¹

The establishment of the headquarters of international organizations in Austria strengthened its connection with the international community, as intended by the government, and its international commitment to humanity and human rights politics through international cooperation. The narrative of a

---

66 UNIDO, permanent headquarters, 22 November 1971, United Nations Archives and Record Management (UNARMS), UNIDO – new headquarters, 1971–1973, S-0290-0024-02.
67 Headquarters of the United Nations Industrial Development Organization, General Assembly A/RES/2212, 22 December 1966, UNARMS, UNIDO – correspondence, 1966–1967, S-0290-0023-08; MRP Nr. 27, 2 December 1966, Beilage F, BMAA, Wahl Wiens zum Amtssitz der neuerrichteten UN-Organisation für Industrielle Entwicklung UNIDO genannt, ÖStA, AdR, BKA, MRP, 2. Republik, Klaus II, Box 251.
68 Knoll/Röhrlich, "neutrale Österreich."
69 Schmidl, "Wien als internationales Zentrum," 714–717; Rauchensteiner, *Unter Beobachtung*, 395–398.
70 United Nations family in Vienna, https://www.unov.org/unov/en/un_in_vienna.html (22 February 2024).
71 Geschichte des Internationalen Zentrums Wien, https://www.unov.org/unov/de/vic_history.html (22 February 2024); Schmidl, "Wien als internationales Zentrum," 715.

humanitarian Austria committed to the values of peace and freedom, as established in 1956, gained high international visibility as it found its expression in the stone and glass of the UN buildings on the east bank of the River Danube.

III. Ambition vs. Reality: Austria's humanitarian aid under revision

Although appealing to a 'humanitarian tradition' and the self-perception as a humanitarian country, Austria's ambitions came with limitations. The following section focuses on examples and arguments that illustrate – without any claim to completeness – the ambivalences in the story of 'humanitarian Austria' from the late 1950s to the beginning of the 1980s. The selection of the examples highlights the ambivalence between humanitarian ambitions and *realpolitik* and were selected for this reason.

First, with respect to Austria's refugee and asylum politics, the narrative of 'humanitarian Austria' was shaped through the interplay between a generous first asylum policy and the government's appeals to other countries to take in refugees. Contrary to the popular narrative, the government's main strategy for solving 'refugee crises' during the Cold War focused on transit instead of asylum. To that end, the various Austrian governments repeatedly requested that the international 'Western' community take in as many refugees as possible.[72] According to the government's argumentation, as already highlighted by then Secretary of State Bruno Kreisky in 1956, Austria was too small to deal with such an influx of refugees alone[73] – a narrative repeatedly used in 'refugee crises' that came after the Hungarian case, such as the 'Czechoslovakian refugee crisis' in 1968/69 and the 'Polish refugee crisis' in 1981/82.[74] When the Austrian government deemed the aid that the international community provided insufficient, politicians publicly criticized the international community. For example, at a meeting of the UNREF Executive Committee in Geneva on 29 January 1957, Austria's minister of the interior, Oskar Helmer (SPÖ), argued Austria could not be "doomed, by virtue of its geographical situation, to bear the main burden of

---

72 Knoll, "Calling."
73 Statement Bruno Kreisky, MRP, Nr. 15, ÖStA, AdR, BKA, MRP, 2. Republik, Raab II, Box 148.
74 For the "Czechoslovakian refugee crises," see Silke Stern, "Die tschechoslowakische Emigration: Österreich als Erstaufnahme- und Asylland," in *Prager Frühling. Das internationale Krisenjahr 1968*, edited by Stefan Karner et al. (Cologne-Weimar-Vienna: Böhlau, 2008), 1025–1043; for the "Polish refugee crises," see Sarah Knoll, "Flucht oder Migration? Polnische Flüchtlinge in Österreich 1981/82," in *Österreich – Polen. Stationen gemeinsamer Geschichte im 20. Jahrhundert*, edited by Wanda Jarzabek and Peter Ruggenthaler (Graz-Vienna: Lykam, 2021), 223–238.

the Hungarian refugee problem," because the "fate of the Hungarian refugees is a matter of the entire free world."[75] Despite such criticism, the international community perceived Austria's treatment of Hungarian refugees in 1956 extremely positively, which helped distract from Austria's policy of becoming a transit country, instead reinforcing the narrative of a humanitarian, charitable Austria.

Second, there was a discrepancy between the discourse of help and Austria's financial contribution to international relief projects. This is evident if we look at Austria's support for UNHCR. During the 1970s, the relationship between UNHCR and the Austrian government, now a solely Social Democratic government under Chancellor Bruno Kreisky, became increasingly strained, although UNHCR was an important partner for the Austrian government while it was dealing with the influx of refugees throughout the 1950s and 1960s.[76] A main reason for this deteriorating relationship was that the Austrian government was unwilling to make more generous financial contributions to UNHCR's programs. UNHCR in Geneva became increasingly critical of Austria's modest contributions.[77] Austrian financial support was indeed low in the late 1970s and early 1980s. In 1978, Austria contributed 50,000 US dollars to UNHCR's general budget, and in 1979 the amount was only raised by 5,000 US dollars to 55,000. In comparison, Italy contributed 1,713,691 US dollars in 1979, New Zealand 287,280 US dollars, Luxembourg 71,642 US dollars, Uganda 241,333 US dollars, and Papua New Guinea 300,000 US dollars.[78]

In 1979, UNHCR asked for an evaluation of Austria's contribution to the budget towards the UN Refugee Agency.[79] These demands were even supported by the Austrian delegation in Geneva, where the UNHCR headquarters are located. The Austrian delegation argued it was important to support UNHCR because of the imperative of international solidarity and the "burden-sharing system," from which Austria had also benefitted during the 'Hungarian refugee crisis' in 1956 and when Czechoslovaks fled to Austria after the invasion of a coalition of the Warsaw Pact on 21 August 1968.[80] The Austrian delegation in

---

75 UNREF Executive Committee 4th Session, Summary Record of the 27th Meeting, Palais des Nations, Geneva, 29 January 1957, United Nations Library & Archives Geneva, United Nations General Assembly, A/AC.79/SR.27, 26 April 1957, 11.
76 Knoll, "Calling," 395–402.
77 Amtsvermerk über das Gespräch des Generalsekretärs des BMAA mit Direktor Homann-Herimberg, no date (presumably 23 December 1981), ÖStA, AdR, BMAA, Sektion II-pol., 1981, Polen 166, GZ. 166.02.40/53-II.3/81, Box. 31.
78 Entwicklung der Beiträge an internationale Organisationen in den Jahren 1978–1981, no date, Kreisky-Archiv, Bestand Bruno Kreisky, VII.1 Länderboxen, Polen, Box 6.
79 BMAA an BKA, z.Hd. BK Bruno Kreisky, Wien 29. Oktober 1979, Kreisky-Archiv, Bestand Bruno Kreisky, VII.1 Länderboxen, Polen, Box 6, Zl. 304.11/70-IV.2/79.
80 Stern, "Die tschechoslowakische Emigration"; see also document in footnote 81.

Geneva agreed Austria was responsible for contributing because of the increased need for aid worldwide.[81] This incident was effective insofar as the Austrian government increased the planned contribution from 60,000 US dollars to 100,000 US dollars in 1980.[82] Compared to UNHCR's estimated budget needs of 250 million dollars for 1980, this was still a very small contribution. The same year, UNHCR in turn planned to spend 125,000 US dollars on local aid programs in Austria.[83] When confronted with this discrepancy, the Austrian federal government primarily justified its small financial contribution to UNHCR's budget with the argument that the country had to shoulder great burdens as a country of first asylum for Eastern European refugees.[84] Especially in 1981 and 1982, the government pointed to the high number of Polish refugees in Austria,[85] which made further contributions to the UNHCR budget impossible.[86] At the same time, however, the Austrian government expected support from UNHCR to deal with the Polish refugees in Austria and their ongoing travel to other countries in 1981/82.[87]

The Austrian government was somewhat more generous when it came to supporting UNHCR resettlement programs, although these were still more symbolic in nature due to their rather modest scope. For example, in 1972 the government agreed to take in 1,740 refugees from Cambodia and Vietnam ('Indochina refugees'), 200 from Chile, 250 from Argentina, and 100 Kurds from Iran. By June 1981, 1,619 asylum seekers from Cambodia and Vietnam, 102 from Iran, 515 from Chile, and 228 from Argentina were staying in Austria within these quotas. In 1972, the government allowed 1,300 people from Uganda to transit through Austria, 200 of whom were offered the opportunity to remain in the country.[88] Despite the rather modest amounts in terms of worldwide refugee protection, it was important to the Austrian federal government and above all Chancellor Bruno Kreisky, head of the Austrian government from 1970 until

---

81 Erik Nettel, Leiter Österreichischen Delegation bei der UNO in Genf, an BMAA, Wien 16. Oktober 1979, Kreisky-Archive, Bestand Bruno Kreisky, VI.8 Minderheiten, Flüchtlinge, Ausländerangelegenheiten, Box 26.
82 Flüchtlings- und Asylpolitik, in *Außenpolitischer Bericht* 1980, edited by BMAA (Vienna: BMAA, 1980), 161.
83 Erik Nettel, Leiter Österreichischen Delegation bei der UNO in Genf, an BMAA, Wien 16. Oktober 1979, Kreisky-Archive, Bestand Bruno Kreisky, VI.8 Minderheiten, Flüchtlinge, Ausländerangelegenheiten, Box 26.
84 BMAA an BKA, z.Hd. BK Bruno Kreisky, Wien 29. Oktober 1979, Kreisky-Archiv, Bestand Bruno Kreisky, VII.1 Länderboxen, Polen, Box 6, Zl. 304.11/70-IV.2/79.
85 Knoll, "Flucht oder Migration."
86 Outgoing Cabel UNHCR Geneva, 14 April 1982, UNHCR-Archive, 100.AUS.POL, Refugees from Poland in Austria 1971–1982 (Vol. 2).
87 Knoll, "Flucht oder Migration," 228–230.
88 Österreich hat seit dem Jahr 1972 auch Asylwerber:innen aus anderen Kontingenten aufgenommen, o.D., Kreisky-Archiv, Bestand Bruno Kreisky, VII.1 Länderboxen, Polen, Box 6.

1983, that Austria "does not lose its credibility as a country of asylum."[89] However, the argument that Austria's "traditional role as a country of first asylum" came with an enormous social, political, and financial burden was once again used to argue against increases in admission quotas for refugees from foreign countries outside Europe.[90]

Third, the mutual offsetting of humanitarian assistance was a constant feature of Austria's humanitarian efforts to avoid more substantial engagement in humanitarian projects – as already seen with the debates about financial contributions to UNHCR. The Austrian government under Bruno Kreisky again used the large number of refugees that were already in the country as an excuse not to participate in aid programs for refugees from African countries in 1981. Consequently, the first International Conference on Assistance to Refugees in Africa (ICARA Conference) took place without the participation of Austria, on 9 and 10 April 1981 at the Palais des Nations, the headquarters of the United Nations in Geneva. Chancellor Kreisky decided that "the request for aid for refugees in Africa cannot be approached, since in view of the increasing services for refugees in Austria, a division of budget funds is not expedient."[91] This decision was criticized by the Department of the Foreign Ministry, which was responsible for contacts with international organizations, in particular the United Nations. For the year 1979, the department calculated that even if "Austria's indirect contributions to the refugee system and the non-refundable costs for the deployment of Austrian contingents to UNFICYP [United Nations Peacekeeping Force in Cyprus] and UNDO [United Nations Disengagement Observer Force]" were included, Austria still spent less on refugees than comparable states with similar economic conditions, such as Denmark and Norway. The report cited 8.5 million US dollars for "indirect" refugee support and 6.2 million US dollars for troop contingents in UN missions.[92] Nonetheless, Austria's expenditure on Polish refugees was the key argument with which the Austrian government justified that it was not willing to make any major financial outlays for development aid or global refugee protection.[93] Chancellor Bruno Kreisky in particular tended to

---

89 Staribacher-Tagebücher, 21. April 1981, https://staribacher.acdh.oeaw.ac.at/ (22 February 2024).
90 BMAA, Vietnamflüchtlinge/Boat People, Arlind Schmidt, Deutsches Komitee Not-Ärzte ev., Wien, 6. April 1982, Kreisky-Archiv, Bestand Bruno Kreisky, VI.8 Minderheiten, Flüchtlinge, Ausländerangelegenheiten, Box 26.
91 Afrika, Flüchtlingskonferenz, österr. Beitrag, BKA and BMAA, Vienna, 14. April 1981, ÖStA, AdR, BMAA, Sektion II-pol., 1981, UNO 423, GZ. 423.05/10-II.5/81, Box 68.
92 Afrika, Flüchtlingskonferenz, österr. Beitrag, Wien, 29. April 1981, ÖStA, AdR, BMAA, Sektion II-pol., 1981, UNO 423, GZ. 423.05/10-II.5/81, Box 68.
93 Staribacher-Tagebücher, 23 February 1982, https://staribacher.acdh.oeaw.ac.at/ (22 February 2024).

offset refugee numbers in the country, financial support for refugee programs, and development aid.[94]

Fourth, the offsetting of humanitarian expenditure also included the construction of the United Nations headquarters in Vienna and involvement in United Nations peacekeeping missions. In the government's quest to minimize state expenditure for international aid, even such prestige projects were used as arguments. In 1981, the secretary-general of the Foreign Ministry, Alois Reitbauer, referred to Austria's expenditure for the construction of the United Nations headquarters in Vienna and Austria's peacekeeping activities to justify the low financial contributions towards UNHCR.[95] Reference to the cost of constructing the new United Nations headquarters was used as an argument not only in relation to the demands of UNHCR. As early as 1967, support for the UNIDO budget was linked to the cost of building the UNIDO headquarters in the city.[96]

Of course, humanitarianism is always a choice. It is politicians who make decisions about whom to help and which projects receive funding. These considerations are always connected to domestic political interests, foreign policy constellations, or global alliance politics. Nevertheless, what is striking about Austria's approach is the constant outweighing of aid. The government did not draw a clear line between refugee support, development aid, peacekeeping missions, or building the UN headquarters. In practice or *realpolitik*, these projects were seen as coherent efforts for a global humanitarian mission.

IV. Conclusion

Defining "humanitarianism" solely from a popular and moral perspective neglects the inherent political dimension of helping others. Humanitarianism is not a one-way street where only the recipients of aid benefit. Rather, the countries giving aid are also influenced by the act of giving and, moreover, use humanitarian projects for their own political interests. In the case of Austria, humanitarianism functioned as a way to create a new, positive self-image of the country which distanced its society from the National Socialist past. The year 1956 was the initial starting point of the narrative of 'humanitarian Austria.' The

---

94 Flüchtlingsstatistiken 1978–1982, Kreisky-Archiv, Bestand Bruno Kreisky, VII.6. Außenpolitik, Cancùn-Gipfel, Nord-Süd-Konflikt, Entwicklungshilfe.
95 Amtsvermerk über das Gespräch des Generalsekretärs des BMAA mit Direktor Homann-Herimberg, no date (presumably 23 December 1981), ÖStA, AdR, BMAA, Sektion II-pol., 1981, Polen 166, GZ. 166.02.40/53-II.3/81, Box 31.
96 Press Release 80/C/54/IDO/1, Austria to contribute $200.000 to UNIDO, 5 January 1967, UNARMS, S-0290-0023-08, UNIDO – correspondence, 1966–1967.

'Hungarian refugee crisis' offered the opportunity to present Austria as a peaceful, democratic, and 'Western'-oriented asylum country to the world. During these few weeks in autumn 1956, a powerful narrative was born which became an important part of how Austria is perceived and perceives itself to this day.

An important factor for the consolidation of this narrative was international organizations setting up their headquarters in Austria. Here, 1956 was once again a key moment. The establishment of the IAEA headquarters in Vienna the same year paved the way for Austria to becoming a place of international exchange. The government's interests in hosting international conferences and organizations and strengthening Austria's international visibility continued in the 1960s. The strategy was successful and, with the arrival of UNIDO in 1967, Vienna became the third official seat of the United Nations. Especially the settlement of UNIDO and the organization's understanding of humanitarianism through technical support gave the Austrian government the opportunity to combine the political strategy of hosting international organizations with the humanitarian narrative created in 1956. What began as the slow construction of a self-image with the support of Hungarian refugees, over time and through the visibility of humanitarian projects and organizations became a tradition that nobody questions today. Nevertheless, to this day, Austria's claims to be a humanitarian country have clashed with the *realpolitik* of the country's domestic and foreign political interests.

Abstracts

To Help or Not to Help – Humanitarianism in the 20th Century

Doina Anca Cretu
The American Red Cross and Visions of Rebuilding of the Balkans after the First World War

This article explores facets of the humanitarian turn of the American Red Cross (ARC) in the Balkans in the immediate aftermath of the First World War. It argues that notions of Balkanism entered the humanitarian vernacular and praxis in the period. ARC relief workers first saw the Balkans as a locale of war-induced need. At the same time, they believed in a long-embedded, yet fixable, Orientalism of Balkan states and their societies. Departing from this dual perception, ARC humanitarians developed visions of the rebuilding of the Balkans through the lens of relief to alleviate the effects of war and in the belief that it would have a civilizing influence on local recipients. This article explores this dichotomy as it maps ARC workers' humanitarian imagination and its practical implications through the lens of famine and disease relief, as well as through agendas of orphan care.
Keywords: Humanitarianism, First World War, Red Cross, Balkans

Katharina Seibert
Springboards for Women's Careers. International Humanitarianism, the Spanish Civil War, and the Rise of Mercedes Milá Nolla

Amidst the Spanish Civil War, in March 1937, Mercedes Milá Nolla was made inspector general of the Female Services in the Health Service of the Francoist army. It was the peak of her career, which began twenty years earlier at the Spanish Red Cross, where she trained to become a bedside nurse. In this paper, her professional trajectory serves as a case study with which to assess humani-

tarianism as a context that enabled female professional careers. While gender historians point to the glass ceiling women still face today in humanitarian organizations, the case of Mercedes Milá shows how she changed lanes from working as a Red Cross nurse to working as the head of all the army nurses. The Spanish Red Cross and its networks with other humanitarian actors served, then, as a springboard that launched her career, and the Spanish Civil War opened the doors for her to become influential in healthcare politics in early Francoism. This paper adds to the historiography of humanitarianism the perspective of gender and class by looking at its entanglements with the professionalization of nursing and national developments in health politics.
Keywords: Spanish Civil War, Francoism, Nursing, Humanitarianism

Julia Schulte-Werning
Milk for the Mellah. Infant Health and the Logistics of Post-Holocaust Humanitarian Aid for Jewish Communities in French Morocco

In May 1953, a new milk station was opened in the Casablanca polyclinic La Maternelle-OSE. It had been set-up by the *American Jewish Joint Distribution Committee* (JDC) and the *Oeuvre de Secours aux Enfants* (OSE) as part of their medical program for impoverished Jewish communities in French-ruled Morocco. Milk powder imported from the United States was turned into bottles for distribution to sick or malnourished infants of the *mellah*, the Jewish quarter of Casablanca. The OSE–JDC campaign and the establishment of the milk station were part of larger Jewish humanitarian efforts in the field of medical aid and community development in Morocco and North Africa after the Holocaust. Tracing the logistics of funding and setting up the milk station highlights the friction between Jewish organizations competing for their respective realms of authority and sheds light on the broader visions tied to providing milk for the infants of the *mellah*. I argue that milk functioned both as a commodity and as a symbol in the post-Holocaust quest to raise a "healthy new generation" in late colonial Morocco and played a central role in positioning Jewish organizations within the landscape of international infant health endeavors.
Keywords: Humanitarian aid, Jewish organizations, Moroccan Jewish history, Milk distribution, Infant health, Postwar Era, Decolonization

Sarah Knoll
Humanitarianism as a Policy Strategy? Revisiting Austria's 'Humanitarian Tradition'

Austria's "humanitarian tradition" has become an inherent part of Austria's self-perception to which politicians and the public refer in different political contexts and periods. But where did this narrative come from and how has it evolved? This paper analyses the question of how humanitarianism has been used as a political strategy by the Austrian government and how this humanitarian narrative shaped Austria's identity and politics. First, the paper looks at the Hungarian refugee crises in 1956 as a point in time when this narrative first gained momentum. It was an event which created a new and positive picture of Austria in contrast to that of the still recent, National Socialist past. Second, it analyses the hosting of international organizations, especially the United Nations Industrial Development Organization (UNIDO), as way of legitimizing the country's independence and connection to the 'West' through a commitment to values of freedom and humanity. Third, it traces the fine line between Austria's humanitarian claims and the *realpolitik* of humanitarian support. Therefore, this paper operates with a definition of "humanitarianism" as an inherently political activity that shaped not "only" the recipients of humanitarian aid mission but also the financial donors.

Keywords: Austria, Hungary 1956, UNO-City, Humanitarian Politics

Reviews

Zuzana Panczová/Gabriela Kiliánová/Tomáš Kubisa, Volkskunde in den Diensten des Dritten Reiches. Deutsche Forscher und Forscherinnen in der Slowakei, Berlin: LIT Verlag 2023, 190 Seiten.

Die Studie beleuchtet die Situation der deutschsprachigen Minderheiten in der Slowakei, die während der NS-Zeit einem „doppelten Druck auf ihre nationale Loyalität" (S. 12) ausgesetzt waren. Zudem wird die Beziehung zwischen Wissenschaft und politischer Ideologie anhand der Geschichte der slowakischen Volkskunde während der NS-Zeit analysiert. Die Disziplin, die sich im 19. Jahrhundert als „Produkt der Romantik und nationaler Bewegungen" (S. 147) formierte, war von Beginn an nicht nur von wissenschaftlicher Neugier, sondern auch von nationalistischem und identitätspolitischem Eifer geprägt. Zunehmend von ‚völkischen' Ideologemen beeinflusst (Kapitel I), verschmolzen bisweilen akademische Aktivitäten und politische Agitation. Das Buch widmet sich zentralen Institutionen und Akteur:innen, die beispielhaft für das Streben nach Erkenntnis über diverse kulturelle Ausdrucksformen stehen. Im nationalsozialistischen Kontext vermengte sich dieses Forschungsinteresse mit propagandistischen Intentionen. Die skizzierten Forschungsunterfangen, die eine Rechtfertigung für territoriale Ansprüche durch die (Über-)Betonung deutscher Kulturleistungen im europäischen Osten liefern sollten, spiegeln die kontroversen Konzepte hinter den Begriffen „Volk", „Nation" und „Staat" und die komplexen Debatten rund um Identität und Zugehörigkeit. Gründlich recherchierte Fallbeispiele vermitteln die akademischen und politischen Entwicklungen und Verstrickungen anschaulich.

Als ein zentraler Akteur trat der Volkskundler Bruno Schier (1902–1984) in Erscheinung, dessen akademische Laufbahn während des Zweiten Weltkrieges an Fahrt gewann. Seine mit der Universität Bratislava assoziierten Forschungsaktivitäten in der Slowakei in den 1940er-Jahren zielten darauf ab, die vermeintliche Vorherrschaft ‚germanisch-deutscher' Kulturtraditionen in Mittelosteuropa hervorzustreichen. Für das NS-Regime waren Schiers Aktivitäten, die mehr und mehr politischer Natur waren, damit von Interesse (Kapitel IV).

Eine institutionelle Schlüsselrolle hatte von 1941 bis 1944 das „Institut für Heimatforschung" (IHF) in Käsmark/Kežmarok (Kapitel II), an dem das Ehepaar Franz J. Beranek (1902–1967), der die Abteilung für Sprachliche Volksforschung leitete, und Hertha Wolf-Beranek (1912–1977), die als Leiterin der Abteilung Volkskunde fungierte, tätig war. Von Reichsstellen und der Deutschen Partei eingesetzt, sollte das IHF die „Gleichschaltung" der deutschsprachigen Minderheiten in der Slowakei vorantreiben und die Vorstellung von der vermeintlichen Überlegenheit der deutschen Kultur in der Region perpetuieren. In diesem Kontext ist besonders Hertha Wolf-Beraneks Rolle interessant. Als berufstätige Akademikerin entsprach sie nicht dem Frauenbild ihrer Zeit, jedoch zeigte sie (möglicherweise gerade deswegen) einen bemerkenswerten Arbeitseifer. Ihre Leistungen, darunter die Einrichtung mehrerer volkskundlicher Archive auf Basis von Fragebogenaktionen, wurden laut zeitgenössischen Quellen wesentlich positiver bewertet als die ihres Mannes (S. 71). Trotzdem hoffte man, nach dem Krieg männliche Forscher für das IHS gewinnen zu können (S. 62). Ein potenzieller Untersuchungsbereich, der eine vertiefende Analyse erfahren könnte, bezieht sich sowohl auf diese festgestellte Paradoxie als auch auf die Gestaltungsspielräume und die Handlungsmacht der Forscherinnen am IHS, einschließlich weiterer Frauen neben Wolf-Beranek, die, im Gegensatz zu ihrem Ehemann, lediglich in einem Unterkapitel porträtiert wird. Ein eigenständiges Kapitel, das diese Aspekte aus einer geschlechterhistorischen Perspektive beleuchtet und die Stellung von Hertha Wolf-Beranek in der Gliederung des Buches adäquater positioniert, hätte weiterführende und erkenntnisreiche Einsichten bringen können. Die dominantere Darstellung von Franz J. Beranek im Buch, trotz der beschriebenen Beurteilung seiner Forschungsleistungen im Vergleich zu seiner Frau, scheint jedoch primär auf die vorhandene Quellenlage zurückzuführen sein.

Der Ausgangspunkt der Forschungsarbeiten war ein Aktenbestand, der über Jahrzehnte unbeachtet am Institut für Ethnologie und Sozialanthropologie der Slowakischen Akademie der Wissenschaften (SAW) in Bratislava aufbewahrt wurde. Die Provenienz der Sammlung ist bis dato nicht abschließend geklärt; wahrscheinlich handelt es sich um die Hinterlassenschaften des Ehepaars Beranek. Ein erheblicher Teil der Dokumente besteht aus Texten wie slowakischen Legenden und Mythen sowie Fragebögen, Bibliografien, Notizen und Korrespondenzen, die Franz J. Beranek zugeordnet werden, der sich am IHS vor allem mit der Dialektforschung in Bezug auf die deutschsprachigen Minderheitengruppen der sogenannten ‚Habaner' und ‚Hunzokaren' beschäftigt hat.

Die klar strukturierte und gut verständliche Darstellung macht das Buch für eine breite Leserschaft zugänglich. Manche Leser:innen würden es jedoch möglicherweise bevorzugen, bereits früher im Text – anstatt erst im dritten Kapitel – Informationen über die Quellenbeschaffenheit zu erhalten, da dies zu einem umfassenderen Verständnis des Kontexts und des gewählten Narrativs beitragen könnte. Weiters wirft die wiederholte Charakterisierung der Volkskunde im NS-Kontext als eher passives Opfer politischer Einflussnahme, besonders in der Einleitung, einen Schatten auf die Frage nach der eigenverantwortlichen und proaktiven Beteiligung der porträtierten Forscher:innen an den propagandistischen Zielen des NS-Regimes. Die Hervorhebung des Missbrauchs (S. 5, S. 35), der Instrumentalisierung (S. 8) und der „ideologische(n) Nutzung" (S. 6) der Disziplin, wenngleich auch diese Realität nicht zu leugnen ist, steht in einer gewissen Diskrepanz zu den Aussagen und Handlungen der Akteur:innen, die durch die präsentierten Quellen belegt sind. Diese lassen tendenziell auf eine bewusste und eigeninitiative Mitwirkung im Dienst dieser Ziele schließen. Die Autor:innen, deren umfassende Analyse von einer tiefgreifenden Kenntnis des Forschungsfeldes zeugt, stellen diese Beteiligung im weiteren Verlauf des Textes differenziert und ausgewogen dar.

Zuzana Panczová studierte Ethnologie und Geschichte an der Comenius-Universität in Bratislava. Ihre Forschung fokussiert sich auf die Analyse von Narrativen wie Gerüchten, Legenden und Verschwörungserzählungen, insbesondere in Bezug auf Gruppenidentität, religiösen Diskurs und Ideologie. Sie ist Senior Research Fellow am Institut für Ethnologie und Sozialanthropologie der Slowakischen Akademie der Wissenschaften und bekleidet seit 2021 das Amt der Vizepräsidentin für internationale Beziehungen. Von 2019 bis 2022 leitete Panczová das VEGA-Projekt „Folklore, Folkloristics and Ideology", das sich weniger erforschten Aspekten der Wissenschaftsgeschichte der Volkskunde in der Slowakei widmete und zur Entstehung des besprochenen Buches beitrug.

Gabriela Kiliánová absolvierte ein Volkskunde-Studium in Bratislava. Bis zu ihrer Emeritierung 2018 war sie am Institut für Ethnologie und Sozialanthropologie der Slowakischen Akademie der Wissenschaften tätig, wo sie zwischen 2000 und 2012 die Position der Institutsdirektorin innehatte. In Anerkennung für ihre Forschung zu kollektiven Identitäten im Kontext von Transformations- und Modernisierungsprozessen, Todesriten, Erzähltraditionen und der Geschichte der Ethnologie in der Slowakei und Mitteleuropa, erhielt sie mehrere slowakische und internationale Forschungspreise, darunter die Medaille der Slowakischen Akademie der Wissenschaften zur Förderung der Wissenschaft im Jahr 2021.

Tomáš Kubisa absolvierte ein Studium in Ethnologie und außereuropäischen Studien in Trnava und Prag. Er ist im Bereich der wissenschaftlichen Sammlungen des Instituts für Ethnologie und Kulturanthropologie der Slowakischen Akademie der Wissenschaften tätig, wo er 2022 seine Promotion abgeschlossen hat. Sowohl Kubisa als auch Kiliánová waren in das oben genannte VEGA-Projekt involviert.

Das Buch, das erfreulicherweise nun in einer überarbeiteten deutschen Fassung vorliegt, stellt einen bedeutenden Beitrag zur Fachgeschichte in der Slowakei sowie zur allgemeineren Geschichte der „Wissenschaften vom Menschen" in Mitteleuropa dar. Die Studie erweist sich als solide Grundlage für weiterführende Forschungen, die beispielsweise an den genannten Anregungen zur Präzisierung bestimmter Nuancen im Text ansetzen könnten.

Lisa Gottschall

Raoul Kneucker/Manfried Welan, Die Fragen des Pilatus. Wahrheit – Gerechtigkeit – Glaube, Graz: Leykam 2023, 112 Seiten.

Die beiden Autoren Raoul F. Kneucker und Manfried Welan stellen in ihrem Buch-Essay „Die Fragen des Pilatus" den Versuch, den Ablauf des historischen Prozesses gegen Jesus zu klären, in den Mittelpunkt. Daneben setzen sie sich auch näher mit den Begrifflichkeiten Wahrheit, Gerechtigkeit und Glaube auseinander. Neben diesem Dreieck steht ihnen zufolge auch die Klärung der Frage, was „wahrer Glaube" ist, im Fokus. Sie arbeiten heraus, dass diesen Fragen nicht nur im historischen Prozess eine Bedeutung zukommt, sondern ein Verständnis nur unter Berücksichtigung des Aspekts möglich ist, dass die drei Begriffe ganz allgemein aufeinander bezogen sind.

Es ist interessant, dass sich Hans Kelsen in den Jahren 1920 und 1953 mit dem historischen Prozess gegen Jesus auseinandergesetzt hat. Die beiden Autoren heben hervor, dass sich das Verständnis der drei Begriffe (Wahrheit, Glaube, Gerechtigkeit) im Lauf der Zeit ändert und von jeder Generation anders gesehen wird. Seit den 1950er-Jahren ist die Forschung zu anderen Schlussfolgerungen gekommen, als dies aus der Perspektive von Kelsen möglich war. Sie nehmen daher eine Kontextualisierung beider Essaystellen vor, um die Beweggründe Kelsens herauszufinden. Diese Kontextualisierung wird aber nur unzureichend hergestellt, denn es fehlt der wichtige Aspekt, Kelsens Auseinandersetzung mit seiner Biografie gerade in diesen beiden Jahren in Bezug zu setzen.

1920, also kurz nach Ende des Ersten Weltkriegs, war Kelsen an der Ausarbeitung der österreichischen Bundesverfassung beteiligt. Insbesondere die bis heute grundlegenden Bestimmungen über die Verfassungsgerichtsbarkeit trugen seine Handschrift. Er war seit 1919 Verfassungsrichter und wurde nach der Umgestaltung des Verfassungsgerichtshofs 1929/1930 nicht wieder zum Richter bestellt. Er übernahm daraufhin Professuren in Köln, Genf und Prag und emigrierte 1940 in die USA. Nach 1945 wurde Kelsen, wie viele andere, nicht zurückgeholt und blieb zeitlebens in Amerika.

Kelsen wird mit der von ihm geprägten Wiener Schule des Rechtspositivismus die Überwindung des Naturrechts zugeschrieben. Damit ist nicht die Abwendung von allgemeinen Rechtsgrundsätzen gemeint, sondern lediglich der Vorrang des gesetzten Rechts, das einem der Willkür entzogenen Erzeugungsprozess unterworfen ist, mit einer nachprüfenden Kontrolle durch den Verfassungsgerichtshof (VfGH), wodurch auch ein umfassender Schutz jeder Minderheit an sich – ein Kelsen besonders wichtiger Aspekt – gewährleistet ist.

In der ersten Republik war Kelsen von Seiten der Christlichsozialen heftigen Anfeindungen ausgesetzt. Er galt als Sympathisant der Sozialisten, stand aber immer über den Parteien und orientierte sich bei all seinen Tätigkeiten ausschließlich am Recht; an dem, was ist, und nicht an dem, was sein soll, wie es im Rechtspositivismus so klar herausgearbeitet wurde.

Die besonders heftig kritisierten VfGH-Entscheidungen betrafen die Gültigkeit der sogenannten „Sever-Ehen" und die Zulässigkeit der Feuerbestattung. Entscheidungen wie diese führten letztlich dazu, dass beim Umbau des VfGH das Amt aller Verfassungsrichter ex lege für erloschen erklärt wurde, wovon auch Kelsen betroffen war.

Über die im Essay enthaltene Wiedergabe der beiden Essaystellen hinaus verdienen diese eine nähere inhaltliche Betrachtung. 1920, bei der ersten Auseinandersetzung Kelsens, lag die weitere Entwicklung der jungen Demokratie noch im Dunklen. Im Jahr des Inkrafttretens des Bundesverfassungsgesetzes sieht Kelsen das Vorgehen des Pilatus als demokratisches Symbol. Pilatus, der nicht weiß, was Wahrheit ist, lässt das Volk entscheiden, was laut Kelsen eigentlich gegen die Demokratie spricht – aber nur dann, wenn sich das Volk seiner politischen Wahrheit so gewiss sei wie Jesus. Nur dann wäre das Blutvergießen zur Durchsetzung der politischen Wahrheit als Ergebnis eines demokratischen Prozesses gerechtfertigt. Bloß weltanschauliche Beweggründe, so Kelsen weiterdenkend, vor allem, wenn sie wahre Absichten verschleiern, ließen das niemals zu, auch nicht, wenn dies der Durchsetzung einer fragwürdigen politischen Agenda dient oder wenn damit Rechte einer bestimmten Gruppe oder einer Minderheit eingeschränkt werden sollen. In dieser Auseinandersetzung Kelsens am Beginn der Ersten Republik spürt man eine starke ethische Grundhaltung und ein Demokratieverständnis, das sich in der politischen Realität der 1920er- und 1930er-Jahre nicht durchgesetzt hat, aber in der ausschließlich am Recht orientierten Rechtsprechung des VfGH bis heute eine konsequente Fortentwicklung findet. Dass die Entscheidungen des VfGH von politischer Tragweite waren und sind, steht dazu in keinem Widerspruch, solange diese klare Positionen beziehen, aber ausschließlich am Recht orientiert sind. Die weitere Entwicklung bis in unsere Gegenwart hat gezeigt, dass diese Ausrichtung der Verfassungsrechtsprechung allgemein anerkannt ist und für eine hohe Akzeptanz des VfGH gesorgt hat.

Die zweite Auseinandersetzung Kelsens im Jahr 1953, überarbeitet 1960, ist wohl im Licht der Katastrophe des Nationalsozialismus und des Zweiten Weltkriegs, aber auch des heraufziehenden Kalten Kriegs zu sehen. Diesmal stellt Kelsen die Vernehmung durch Pilatus in den Mittelpunkt, genauer die Aussage Jesus', er sei auf die Welt gekommen, um Zeugnis zu geben für die Wahrheit. Es ist diese Aussage, die Pilatus zu seiner berühmten Frage „Was ist Wahrheit?" veranlasst – wie auch Kelsen –, ohne eine Antwort zu erwarten, ohne sie aber auch zu bekommen, denn Wahrheit sei es gar nicht gewesen, wofür Jesus Zeugnis geben wollte. In der Deutung Kelsens war Jesus geboren, Zeugnis zu geben für die Gerechtigkeit, die er im Königreich Gottes verwirklichen wollte, für diese sei er auch am Kreuz gestorben. Hinter diesem Tod erhebe sich daher die ewige Frage, was diese Gerechtigkeit denn sei. Kelsen schließt damit, diese Frage sei auch nach Ansicht der großen Philosophen nicht beantwortbar, auch wenn dafür in der Welt viel Blut geflossen sei. So knapp und präzise kann man die im Titel des Essays angesprochene Frage des Pilatus beantworten.

Überzeugend ist im Weiteren die juristisch fundierte Analyse des Prozesses selbst, mit Pilatus als zuständigem Richter und daher den Autoren zufolge allein für die Kreuzigung verantwortlich, mag er auch den Hohen Rat als Ankläger (und nicht das Volk als diffuses Ganzes ohne rechtliche Stellung im Verfahren) angehört haben. Den Juden kann daher die Schuld am Kreuzestod nicht untergeschoben werden, so die Autoren ganz klar und eindeutig. Sie belegen den Weg des Pontius ins sprichwörtliche Credo als eine Umdeutung der Spätantike und des Frühmittelalters, mit der den Juden die Verantwortung zugeschoben und gleichzeitig die Rolle des Pilatus beschönigt werden sollte. Die Autoren benennen diese Ursprünge des christlichen Antisemitismus ganz klar und zweifelsfrei.

Interessant ist auch die Auseinandersetzung mit neueren Gerechtigkeitstheorien, in denen sich der Schwerpunkt von reiner Verfahrensgerechtigkeit aktuell wieder stärker zu inhaltlichen Fragen verlagert, insbesondere wenn es um soziale oder wirtschaftliche Aspekte geht.

Die Autoren schließen mit einem Appell für neu auszuhandelnde Sozialkontrakte, um die großen Probleme, vor denen Europa, vor denen die Welt steht, auch im Interesse künftiger Generationen in den Griff zu bekommen. Um diese Wahrheit geht es ihnen zufolge letztlich, um nichts anderes als Gerechtigkeit geht es, ein gutes Leben für die größtmögliche Zahl an Menschen, falls es dafür noch nicht zu spät ist.

Das kundige und tiefschürfende Werk wirft wichtige Fragen auf und gibt, was bei derartigen Auseinandersetzungen nicht immer der Fall ist, weitgehend Antwort. Kelsen selbst wird dabei allerdings nicht übertroffen.

Nikolaus Lehner

Authors

Dr.ⁱⁿ Doina Anca Cretu
Assistant Professor in Modern European History at University of Warwick, UK, ancadoinacretu@gmail.com

Dr.ⁱⁿ Katharina Seibert
Historian and PostDoc Researcher at the Department of Contemporary History, University of Tübingen, katharina.seibert@uni-tuebingen.de

Julia Schulte-Werning, MA
PraeDoc Researcher at the Department of History and Fellow of the Doctoral School for Historical and Cultural Studies, University of Vienna, julia.schulte-werning@univie.ac.at

Dr.ⁱⁿ Sarah Knoll, MA
Historian and PostDoc Researcher at the Department of History, Section Contemporary History, University of Graz, sarah.knoll@uni-graz.at

Zitierregeln

Bei der Einreichung von Manuskripten, über deren Veröffentlichung im Laufe eines doppelt anonymisierten Peer Review Verfahrens entschieden wird, sind unbedingt die Zitierregeln einzuhalten. Unverbindliche Zusendungen von Manuskripten als word-Datei an: verein.zeitgeschichte@univie.ac.at

I. Allgemeines

Abgabe: elektronisch in Microsoft Word DOC oder DOCX.

Textlänge: 60.000 Zeichen (inklusive Leerzeichen und Fußnoten), Times New Roman, 12 Punkt, 1 ½-zeilig. Zeichenzahl für Rezensionen 6.000–8.200 Zeichen (inklusive Leerzeichen).

Rechtschreibung: Grundsätzlich gilt die Verwendung der neuen Rechtschreibung mit Ausnahme von Zitaten.

II. Format und Gliederung

Kapitelüberschriften und – falls gewünscht – Unterkapiteltitel deutlich hervorheben mittels Nummerierung. Kapitel mit römischen Ziffern [I. Literatur], Unterkapitel mit arabischen Ziffern [1.1 Dissertationen] nummerieren, maximal bis in die dritte Ebene untergliedern [1.1.1 Philologische Dissertationen]. Keine Interpunktion am Ende der Gliederungstitel.

Keine Silbentrennung, linksbündig, Flattersatz, keine Leerzeilen zwischen Absätzen, keine Einrückungen; direkte Zitate, die länger als vier Zeilen sind, in einem eigenen Absatz (ohne Einrückung, mit Gänsefüßchen am Beginn und Ende).

Zahlen von null bis zwölf ausschreiben, ab 13 in Ziffern. Tausender mit Interpunktion: 1.000. Wenn runde Zahlen wie zwanzig, hundert oder dreitausend nicht in unmittelbarer Nähe zu anderen Zahlenangaben in einer Textpassage aufscheinen, können diese ausgeschrieben werden.

Daten ausschreiben: „1930er" oder „1960er-Jahre" statt „30er" oder „60er Jahre".

Datumsangaben: In den Fußnoten: 4.3.2011 [keine Leerzeichen nach den Punkten, auch nicht 04.03.2011 oder 4. März 2011]; im Text das Monat ausschreiben [4. März 2011].

Personennamen im Fließtext bei der Erstnennung immer mit Vor- und Nachnamen.

Namen von Organisationen im Fließtext: Wenn eindeutig erkennbar ist, dass eine Organisation, Vereinigung o. Ä. vorliegt, können die Anführungszeichen weggelassen werden: „Die Gründung des Oesterreichischen Alpenvereins erfolgte 1862." „Als Mitglied im Womens Alpine Club war ihr die Teilnahme gestattet." **Namen von Zeitungen/Zeitschriften** etc. siehe unter „Anführungszeichen".

Anführungszeichen im Fall von Zitaten, Hervorhebungen und bei Erwähnung von Zeitungen/Zeitschriften, Werken und Veranstaltungstiteln im Fließtext immer doppelt: „"

Einfache Anführungszeichen nur im Fall eines Zitats im Zitat: „Er sagte zu mir: ‚….'"

Klammern: Gebrauchen Sie bitte generell runde Klammern, außer in Zitaten für Auslassungen: […] und Anmerkungen: [Anm. d. A.].

Formulieren Sie **bitte geschlechtsneutral bzw. geschlechtergerecht.** Verwenden Sie im ersteren Fall bei Substantiven das Binnen-I („ZeitzeugInnen"), nicht jedoch in Komposita („Bürgerversammlung" statt „BürgerInnenversammlung").

Darstellungen und Fotos als eigene Datei im jpg-Format (mind. 300 dpi) einsenden. Bilder werden schwarz-weiß abgedruckt; die Rechte an den abgedruckten Bildern sind vom Autor/von der Autorin einzuholen. Bildunterschriften bitte kenntlich machen: Abb.: Spanische Reiter auf der Ringstraße (Quelle: Bildarchiv, ÖNB).

Abkürzungen: Bitte Leerzeichen einfügen: vor % oder €/zum Beispiel z. B./unter anderem u. a.

Im Text sind möglichst wenige allgemeine Abkürzungen zu verwenden.

III. Zitation

Generell keine Zitation im Fließtext, auch keine Kurzverweise. Fußnoten immer mit einem Punkt abschließen.

Die nachfolgenden Hinweise beziehen sich auf das Erstzitat von Publikationen.
Bei weiteren Erwähnungen sind Kurzzitate zu verwenden.
- Wird hintereinander aus demselben Werk zitiert, bitte den Verweis **Ebd./ebd.** bzw. mit anderer Seitenangabe **Ebd., 12./ebd., 12.** gebrauchen (kein Ders./Dies.), analog: Vgl. ebd.; vgl. ebd., 12.
- Zwei Belege in einer Fußnote mit einem **Strichpunkt;** trennen: Gehmacher, Jugend, 311; Dreidemy, Kanzlerschaft, 29.
- Bei Übernahme von direkten Zitaten aus der Fachliteratur **Zit. n./zit. n.** verwenden.
- Indirekte Zitate werden durch **Vgl./vgl.** gekennzeichnet.

Monografien: Vorname und Nachname, Titel, Ort und Jahr, Seitenangabe [ohne „S."].

Beispiel Erstzitat: Johanna Gehmacher, Jugend ohne Zukunft. Hitler-Jugend und Bund Deutscher Mädel in Österreich vor 1938, Wien 1994, 311.

Beispiel Kurzzitat: Gehmacher, Jugend, 311.
Bei mehreren AutorInnen/HerausgeberInnen: Dachs/Gerlich/Müller (Hg.), Politiker, 14.

Reihentitel: Claudia Hoerschelmann, Exilland Schweiz. Lebensbedingungen und Schicksale österreichischer Flüchtlinge 1938 bis 1945 (Veröffentlichungen des Ludwig-Boltzmann-Institutes für Geschichte und Gesellschaft 27), Innsbruck/Wien [bei mehreren Ortsangaben Schrägstrich ohne Leerzeichen] 1997, 45.

Dissertation: Thomas Angerer, Frankreich und die Österreichfrage. Historische Grundlagen und Leitlinien 1945-1955, phil. Diss., Universität Wien 1996, 18-21 [keine ff. und f. für Seitenangaben, von-bis mit Gedankenstich ohne Leerzeichen].

Diplomarbeit: Lucile Dreidemy, Die Kanzlerschaft Engelbert Dollfuß' 1932-1934, Dipl. Arb., Université de Strasbourg 2007, 29.

Ohne AutorIn, nur HerausgeberIn: Beiträge zur Geschichte und Vorgeschichte der Julirevolte, hg. im Selbstverlag des Bundeskommissariates für Heimatdienst, Wien 1934, 13.

Unveröffentlichtes Manuskript: Günter Bischof, Lost Momentum. The Militarization of the Cold War and the Demise of Austrian Treaty Negotiations, 1950-1952 (unveröffentlichtes Manuskript), 54-55. Kopie im Besitz des Verfassers.

Quellenbände: Foreign Relations of the United States, 1941, vol. II, hg.v. United States Department of States, Washington 1958.
[nach Erstzitation mit der gängigen Abkürzung: FRUS fortfahren].

Sammelwerke: Herbert Dachs/Peter Gerlich/Wolfgang C. Müller (Hg.), Die Politiker. Karrieren und Wirken bedeutender Repräsentanten der Zweiten Republik, Wien 1995.

Beitrag in Sammelwerken: Michael Gehler, Die österreichische Außenpolitik unter der Alleinregierung Josef Klaus 1966-1970, in: Robert Kriechbaumer/Franz Schausberger/Hubert Weinberger (Hg.), Die Transformation der österreichischen Gesellschaft und die Alleinregierung Klaus (Veröffentlichung der Dr.-Wilfried Haslauer-Bibliothek, Forschungsinstitut für politisch-historische Studien 1), Salzburg 1995, 251-271, 255-257.
[bei Beiträgen grundsätzlich immer die Gesamtseitenangabe zuerst, dann die spezifisch zitierten Seiten].

Beiträge in Zeitschriften: Florian Weiß, Die schwierige Balance. Österreich und die Anfänge der westeuropäischen Integration 1947-1957, in: Vierteljahrshefte für Zeitgeschichte 42 (1994) 1, 71-94.
[Zeitschrift Jahrgang/Bandangabe ohne Beistrichtrennung und die Angabe der Heftnummer oder der Folge hinter die Klammer ohne Komma].

Presseartikel: Titel des Artikels, Zeitung, Datum, Seite.
Der Ständestaat in Diskussion, Wiener Zeitung, 5.9.1946, 2.

Archivalien: Bericht der Österr. Delegation bei der Hohen Behörde der EGKS, Zl. 2/pol/57, Fritz Kolb an Leopold Figl, 19.2.1957. Österreichisches Staatsarchiv (ÖStA), Archiv der Republik (AdR), Bundeskanzleramt (BKA)/AA, II-pol, International 2 c, Zl. 217.301-pol/57 (GZl. 215.155-pol/57); Major General Coleman an Kirkpatrick, 27.6.1953. The National Archives (TNA), Public Record Office (PRO), Foreign Office (FO) 371/103845, CS 1016/205 [prinzipiell zuerst das Dokument mit möglichst genauer Bezeichnung, dann das Archiv, mit Unterarchiven, -verzeichnissen und Beständen; bei weiterer Nennung der Archive bzw. Unterarchive können die Abkürzungen verwendet werden].

Internetquellen: Autor so vorhanden, Titel des Beitrags, Institution, URL: (abgerufen Datum). Bitte mit rechter Maustaste den Hyperlink entfernen, so dass der Link nicht mehr blau unterstrichen ist.
Yehuda Bauer, How vast was the crime, Yad Vashem, URL: http://www1.yadvashem.org/yv/en/holocaust/about/index.asp (abgerufen 28. 2. 2011).

Film: Vorname und Nachname des Regisseurs, Vollständiger Titel, Format [z. B. 8 mm, VHS, DVD], Spieldauer [Film ohne Extras in Minuten], Produktionsort/-land Jahr, Zeit [Minutenangabe der zitierten Passage].
Luis Buñuel, Belle de jour, DVD, 96 min., Barcelona 2001, 26:00–26:10 min.

Interview: InterviewpartnerIn, InterviewerIn, Datum des Interviews, Provenienz der Aufzeichnung.
Interview mit Paul Broda, geführt von Maria Wirth, 26. 10. 2014, Aufnahme bei der Autorin.

Die englischsprachigen Zitierregeln sind online verfügbar unter: https://www.verein-zeitgeschichte.univie.ac.at/fileadmin/user_upload/p_verein_zeitgeschichte/zg_Zitierregeln_engl_2018.pdf

Es können nur jene eingesandten Aufsätze Berücksichtigung finden, die sich an die Zitierregeln halten!